The Developmental Process of Japanese Elementary School Teachers Associated with Teaching English while Engaged in Lesson Study

Akiko Kambaru

Acknowledgements

This book is a revision of my doctoral thesis submitted at Kumamoto University in 2017. The revision includes rewording and condensing of the contents. I would like to thank Professor Terry Laskowski, my academic supervisor, for his supervision of this thesis. Professor Laskowski consistently gave me timely knowledge, advice, and direction throughout my research so that I could complete this study. Through his clear explanations, I was able to learn a great deal about qualitative approaches. I am deeply grateful for his enduring patience. I would also like to thank all the professors at Kumamoto University for their kind support and instruction, especially my assistant academic supervisor, Professor Toru Yamashita. I would also like to thank the participants of this study. They allowed me to observe their lessons, join in their discussions, and conduct interviews so that I could finish this study. Finally, I would like to thank my family. I could not have completed this study without their support. Thank you very much. The publication of this book is supported in part by Grant-in Aid from Tsuru University.

Table of Contents

Chapter 1　Introduction ·············· 11

1.1 Motivation of this study ··············11

1.2 Purpose of this study ··············13

1.3 Outline of this study ··············13

1.4 Summary of chapter ··············15

Chapter 2　Literature review ·············· 16

2.1 Research on teaching English in elementary schools ···16

2.1.1 Teaching English in elementary schools ··············16

2.1.2 Research on in-service teachers ··············19

2.1.3 Research on pre-service teachers ··············20

2.2 Research on teachers' thinking in professional development···20

2.2.1 Teachers' thinking ··············21

2.2.2 Teachers' beliefs ··············23

2.2.3 Teacher autonomy ··············24

2.2.4 Research on in-service teachers' thinking ··············25

2.2.5 Research on pre-service teachers' thinking ··············26

2.3 Research on lesson study ··············27

2.3.1 Lesson study ··············27

2.3.2 The international spread of lesson study ··············31

2.3.3 Lesson study as teacher collaboration ··············32

2.3.4 Lesson study and reflection ··············33

2.3.5 Lesson study and action research ··············34

2.3.6 The need for more research documented in Japan 36

2.3.7 Recent problem with lesson study in Japan 37

2.3.8 Research on lesson study pertaining to teaching English in elementary schools 38

2.4 Methodological perspectives and paradigms 38

2.4.1 Perspectives and paradigms 38

2.4.2 Taking a qualitative approach 40

2.4.3 Grounded theory approach (GTA) 40

2.5 Summary of chapter 45

Chapter 3 Methodology 46

3.1 Modified grounded theory approach (M-GTA) 46

3.2 Analysis procedure of M-GTA 48

3.3 Validity and reliability 50

3.4 Summary of chapter 52

Chapter 4 Study on pre-service teachers 53

4.1 About the school 53

4.2 Participants 53

4.3 The teaching practicum schedule 54

4.4 Data collection and analysis 57

4.5 Results and discussion 60

4.5.1 Category (1) [Children's ways of learning English] 62

4.5.1.1 Concept of <Listening> 62

4.5.1.2 Concept of <Alphabet> 63

4.5.1.3 Concept of <Guessing> 64

4.5.1.4 Concept of <Grammar> 66

4.5.2 Category (2) [English knowledge] ·············67

4.5.3 Category (3) [Instructional knowledge] ·············69

    4.5.3.1 Concept of <Flexibility> ·············69

    4.5.3.2 Concept of <Time control> ·············71

    4.5.3.3 Concept of <Understanding children's situations> ·············72

4.5.4 Category (4) [Importance of English use] ·············74

    4.5.4.1 Concept of <A lot of English> ·············74

    4.5.4.2 Concept of <Anxiety> ·············75

4.5.5 Category (5) [Purpose of Foreign Language Activities] ·············77

    4.5.5.1 Concept of <Understanding communication> ·············77

    4.5.5.2 Concept of <Only songs and games> ·············79

    4.5.5.3 Concept of <Course of Study> ·············79

4.5.6 Category (6) [Collegiality] ·············81

    4.5.6.1 Concept of <Deepen one's thoughts> ·············81

    4.5.6.2 Concept of <Help each other> ·············83

    4.5.6.3 Concept of <Positive feeling> ·············83

4.6 Summary of chapter ·············**86**

Chapter 5 Preliminary study on in-service teachers ··· 87

5.1 About the school ·············**87**

5.2 Procedures of the school-based lesson study ·············**90**

5.3 Research lesson and post-lesson discussion ·············**92**

5.4 Findings ·············**93**

  5.4.1 Leadership and shared roles ·············93

  5.4.2 All teachers give their own research lesson every year ·············94

  5.4.3 Informal voluntary meetings ·············95

5.5 Summary of chapter ·············**96**

Chapter 6 Study on in-service teachers ················ 97

6.1 About the school ···············97

6.2 Participants ···············98

6.3 Procedures of the school-based lesson study ···············99

6.4 In-service teachers' views on teaching English ···············102

6.4.1 Data collection and analysis ···············102

6.4.2 Results and discussion ···············104

6.4.2.1 Category (1) [Really needed?] ···············105

6.4.2.1.1 Concept of <Concerning with other subjects> ···········106

6.4.2.1.2 Concept of <Repelling top-down manner> ···············107

6.4.2.2 Category (2) [Anxiety] ···············109

6.4.2.3 Category (3) [Internationalization] ···············111

6.4.2.4 Category (4) [Ideal lesson] ···············112

6.4.2.5 Category (5) [Want to learn HRT's roles in TT] ···········113

6.4.2.5.1 Concept of <No image> ···············114

6.4.2.5.2 Concept of <Good learner model> ···············115

6.4.2.5.3 Concept of <Demonstration> ···············115

6.4.2.6 Category (6) [Assistance] ···············116

6.4.2.6.1 Concept of <ALTs are needed> ···············116

6.4.2.6.2 Concept of <Manuals are needed> ···············118

6.4.3 Summary of teachers' views on teaching English ···············120

6.5 Descriptions of lesson study cycles in this school ···············120

6.5.1 Lesson study 1 ···············120

6.5.1.1 Planning discussion ···············120

6.5.1.2 Research lesson ···············121

6.5.1.3 Post-lesson discussion ···············122

6.5.2 Lesson study 2 ···············126

6.5.2.1 Planning discussion ···········126

6.5.2.2 Research lesson ···········127

6.5.2.3 Post-lesson discussion ···········128

6.5.3 Lesson study 3 ···········131

6.5.3.1 Planning discussion ···········131

6.5.3.2 Research lesson ···········132

6.5.3.3 Post-lesson discussion ···········132

6.5.4 Summary of the descriptions of lesson study cycles in this school
···········134

6.6 The developmental process of in-service teachers ···········**135**

6.6.1 Data collection and analysis ···········135

6.6.2 Results and discussion ···········138

6.6.2.1 Category (1) [Learning in the same context] ···········139

6.6.2.2 Category (2) [Understanding] ···········141

6.6.2.2.1 Concept of <HRT's roles in TT> ···········142

6.6.2.2.2 Concept of <Classroom English> ···········143

6.6.2.3 Category (3) [New perspectives] ···········144

6.6.2.3.1 Concept of <Critical views toward ALTs> ···········145

6.6.2.3.2 Concept of <Applying pedagogical knowledge> ···········147

6.6.2.4 Category (4) [Positive attitude] ···········148

6.6.2.4.1 Concept of <Want to learn English more> ···········148

6.6.2.4.2 Concept of <Want to teach by oneself> ···········150

6.6.3 Summary of the developmental process of in-service teachers
···········153

6.7 Summary of chapter ···········**153**

Chapter 7 Discussion ·············· 155

7.1 Developmental process of pre-service teachers (research question 1)
·············156

7.2 In-service teachers' views on teaching English (research question 2)
·············159

7.3 Developmental process of in-service teachers (research question 3)
·············161

7.4 In-service teachers compared with pre-service teachers ···162

7.5 Additional findings from this study ·············164

    7.5.1 MKO ·············164

    7.5.2 TT with ALTs ·············165

7.6 Summary of chapter ·············166

Chapter 8 Conclusion ·············· 167

8.1 Summary of the study ·············167

8.2 Theoretical implications ·············169

8.3 Pedagogical implications ·············169

8.4 Contributions of the study ·············170

8.5 Limitations of the study and directions for future study ···172

8.6 Concluding statement ·············172

References ·············· 174

Appendices ·············· 191

1. Selected analysis worksheet on pre-service teachers ·············191

2. Frequent words in the data of pre-service teachers according to KH
coder Version 2 ·············192

3. Co-occurrence networks in the data of pre-service teachers according to

KH coder Version 2 ············194

4. Selected analysis worksheet on in-service teachers' views ············195

5. Frequent words in the data of in-service teachers' views according to KH coder Version 2 ············196

6. Co-occurrence networks in the data of in-service teachers' views according to KH coder Version 2 ············198

7. Selected analysis worksheet on the developmental process of in-service teachers ············199

8. Frequent words in the data of in-service teachers' developmental process according to KH coder Version 2 ············200

9. Co-occurrence networks in the data of in-service teachers' developmental process according to KH coder Version 2 ············202

Index ············ **203**

List of Tables

Table 2.1 Comparison of Lesson Study and Traditional Teacher Development
............33

Table 4.1 Background of the Pre-Service Teachers 54

Table 5.1 The Years of Teaching Experience among the Full-Time Teachers at the School (2012-2013 academic year) 88

Table 5.2 Number of Teachers in English Team and Japanese Team per Grade Level 89

Table 5.3 Schedule for a Research Lesson and a Post-Lesson Discussion ···92

Table 6.1 Background of the In-service Teachers 99

Table 6.2 Procedures of the School-Based Lesson Study and of this Study
............100

List of Figures

Figure 2.1. Lesson study cycle including studying curriculum and formulating goals, planning, conducting a research lesson, and reflecting
............29

Figure 4.1. The developmental process of pre-service teachers 61

Figure 5.1. Structure of the school research organization (Preliminary Study)
............89

Figure 6.1. Structure of the school research organization 98

Figure 6.2. In-service teachers' views on teaching English 105

Figure 6.3. The developmental process of in-service teachers 139

Figure 7.1. The relationship among pedagogical content knowledge, pedagogical knowledge, and content knowledge 157

Chapter 1

Introduction

This study focuses on the developmental process of Japanese elementary school teachers as it pertains to teaching English while engaged in lesson study. This chapter outlines the context that led to the study. First, I explain the reasons for my interest in conducting this study. Second, I present what the study aims to do and what questions it addresses. Third, I give an outline of each chapter.

1.1 Motivation of this study

Teaching English in elementary schools is a new concept in the national curriculum of Japan. English is currently taught mostly by homeroom teachers (HRTs) who have not had proper training regarding English language instruction. The inclusion of teaching English has put immense pressure on teachers to make changes in their instruction, as they are expected to meet the curriculum demands. As a teacher educator, I have offered advice and given workshops to elementary school teachers to help them improve their teaching. However, there are still many teachers who have not had any training in teaching English. The actual situation for these teachers is not entirely clear because almost all research articles have studied teachers who already have a lot of experience teaching English. In order to develop a deeper understanding,

I needed to investigate teachers who have had less training and experience teaching English. This need was the inspiration for this study.

In addition, in this study I also report on the developmental process of elementary school pre-service teachers related to their experience teaching English. There is little research on pre-service teachers teaching English, particularly during their teaching practicums. Therefore, research on pre-service teachers going through their teaching practicums with a focus on teaching English is included in the study.

For this study, school-based lesson study is adopted as an effective framework for teacher development. It is the most common form of professional teacher development in Japan (Lewis, 2000; Lewis & Tsuchida, 1998; Murata & Takahashi, 2002; Takahashi, 2000; Takahashi & Yoshida, 2004; Yoshida, 1999). I would like to document lesson study because although lesson study is spreading internationally, there are very few published studies on lesson study conducted in Japan in English. Regarding this point, a preliminary examination of lesson study is also documented in this study to show the reader a typical case example of lesson study.

Over the course of this study, I was in several professional positions. Firstly, I was a teacher at a public elementary school until 2012. In 2012, I conducted the preliminary study about lesson study at that elementary school (see Chapter 5). I was also a participant in that lesson study. I then became a teacher at an elementary school attached to an education university in 2013. During that year, I researched pre-service teachers' teaching practicums (see Chapter 4) and I also served as an HRT and an instructor for such practicums. Finally, in 2014, I became a lecturer at a university. I was an advisor for in-service teachers and in this capacity, in 2015, I researched in-service teachers' lesson study (see Chapter 6).

1.2 Purpose of this study

The purposes of this study are outlined below:

1. To investigate the developmental process of pre-service and in-service teachers as it pertains to their experiences teaching English while engaged in lesson study.
2. To document lesson study conducted in Japan in English.

This study attempts to address the following research questions:

1. How do pre-service teachers develop in terms of teaching English over the course of their teaching practicums while engaged in lesson study?
2. How do in-service teachers view the inclusion of English in the national curriculum?
3. How do in-service teachers develop in terms of teaching English during school-based lesson study?

Next, the outline of each chapter is presented.

1.3 Outline of this study

In Chapter 2, an attempt is made to draw on four particular areas of antecedent literature that are fundamental to the direction taken in this study. First, the discussion focuses on teaching English in elementary schools. English in elementary schools is a new concept in the national curriculum in Japan, and it has implications for elementary school teachers. Research has revealed that teachers struggle with teaching English. Secondly, in order to explore and interpret its impact on teachers and to seek ways to help them in their professional development, issues concerning teachers' thinking are addressed. Teachers' reflections on their thought processes are a very important indicator that can be used to help interpret teacher development. Thirdly, lesson study is reviewed. Lesson study is the most common form of professional development in Japan. School-based lesson study with the entire faculty is the most common type. Finally, methodological perspectives and paradigms are addressed.

In Chapter 3, the methodology for the study is presented. Teachers' voices are seminal to understanding their developmental process. Thus, the data collection is based on discussions during lesson study and interviews. The study is an exploratory attempt to understand teachers' thinking and is not intended to test hypotheses in the experimental tradition. The data analysis is based on methods applied using a modified grounded theory approach (M-GTA) (Kinoshita, 2003, 2007). The findings are conceptualized from the data.

In Chapter 4, the study on the developmental process of pre-service teachers is described. Over the course of their teaching practicums, during the process of going through lesson study, the participants showed a gain in their development in terms of an increase in their knowledge and skills regarding teaching English.

In Chapter 5, the preliminary study on in-service teachers' lesson study is presented. I document procedures of typical school-based lesson study as it takes place in schools, and I report findings from that examination, including three factors that appear to indicate the importance of stressing the value of making lesson study collaborative.

In Chapter 6, the study on the developmental process of in-service teachers associated with their experiences in teaching English while engaged in school-based lesson study is described. First, the teachers' views on teaching English in elementary schools are presented. Then I describe their three lesson study cycles. Finally, the teachers' developmental process is presented.

In Chapter 7, I discuss the results from Chapters 4 and 6. After answers to the three research questions are addressed, a comparative analysis between pre-service teachers and in-service teachers is carried out, including a discussion of commonalities and differences. Additional findings from this study are then addressed.

In Chapter 8, I summarize the entire study. Theoretical implications, pedagogical implications, contributions of the study, limitations, and future directions are then illustrated.

1.4 Summary of chapter

I undertook this study in order to investigate the developmental process of Japanese elementary school teachers as it pertains to their experiences in teaching English while engaged in lesson study. The reason for conducting the study, the research questions, and an outline of each chapter were presented in this chapter. In the next chapter, I review literature in the field to provide context for the study. Four areas of literature are reviewed: teaching English in elementary schools in Japan, teachers' thinking, lesson study, and methodological perspectives and paradigms.

Chapter 2

Literature review

In this chapter, I provide the reader insights into previous research undertaken in this field. First, the discussion focuses on teaching English in elementary schools in Japan. Second, teachers' thinking as a very important indicator to interpret their developmental process is presented. Third, lesson study is reviewed. Finally, methodological perspectives and paradigms are addressed.

2.1 Research on teaching English in elementary schools

In this section, I address English Education in elementary schools. English education in elementary schools is a new concept in the national curriculum of Japan. Research has revealed that teachers struggle with teaching English.

2.1.1 Teaching English in elementary schools

English education in public elementary schools in Japan began in 1992. Starting in that academic year (April-March 1992), only pilot schools implemented English lessons. However, in 2002, schools were authorized to teach English in what was called "the Period for Integrated Studies." The purpose was not to "teach" English, but rather to provide a period of "fun" time in English and to promote familiarity with communicating with people from foreign countries (Kusumoto, 2008). The Japanese Ministry of Education, Culture, Sports, Science and Technology (MEXT) did not dictate content or the amount of time in terms of teaching hours that should be dedicated to these studies. The decision of whether or not to introduce English in the classrooms and what to teach depended on the local governments' and individual schools' choice (Butler, 2004). Some schools conducted English lessons, but others did not. There were no official guidelines for the elementary school English curriculum, which meant that each school or HRT could decide on what to teach (Watanabe, 2006). There were also no course books. Teachers had to spend tremendous amounts of time planning lessons and developing teaching materials (Kusumoto, 2008). Many schools relied on assistant language teachers (ALT, native English speakers introduced through the government-sponsored Japanese Exchange and Teaching [JET] programs or through privately-run dispatch companies) to plan and conduct lessons.

In 2011, English became a compulsory part of the curriculum as Foreign Language Activities for 5th and 6th grade students. The objective of Foreign Language Activities as written in the national curriculum Course of Study emphasizes a focus on communication, and nothing is stated about putting a priority on grammatical structures, as described below:

> To form the foundation of pupils' communication abilities through foreign languages while developing the understanding of languages and cultures through various experiences, fostering a positive attitude toward communication, and familiarizing pupils with the sounds and basic expressions of foreign languages. (MEXT, 2010, p. 1)

Although it is referred to as Foreign Language Activities, English is the language that is expected to be implemented (MEXT, 2010), and instruction is mainly focused on listening and speaking. The annual number of lessons is 35 (one lesson per week), with each lasting 45 minutes. The total number of lessons is 70 over the course of two years (5th & 6th grades). MEXT distributed supplemental books named "Eigo Note" (2009-2011) and "Hi, friends!" (2012-) to pupils, and teacher's manuals with CDs and DVD-ROMs to teachers (Nakajima & Okazaki, 2013). Although teachers are not required to utilize them (Kusumoto, 2008), most teachers do so because they can offer teachers direction on what and how to teach, as well as some teaching materials. Foreign Language Activities is compulsory, but is not treated as an official subject. No grading is conducted (Kusumoto, 2008). Guidelines suggest that English at the elementary school level should be "experiential learning activities" (MEXT, 2007). Despite the fact that the program was implemented in 2011, many current teachers have not yet had appropriate training in teaching English and therefore, experience significant anxiety about their abilities in this regard.

MEXT revised the Course of Study for elementary schools in Japan in March 2017. Under the new policy, MEXT will upgrade English to an official subject for the 5th and 6th grades and require 70 lessons per year (two lessons per week) starting in 2020. Henceforth, not only will listening and speaking be covered over the course of these 70 lessons, but so will reading and writing. In addition, English lessons will commence in the 3rd grade, at 35 lessons per year (one lesson per week). Transition toward the smooth implementation of the new Course of Study began in 2018. During this year, elementary schools are required to conduct at least 15 lessons per year for the 3rd and 4th grades, and at least 50 lessons per year for the 5th and 6th grades. The need for teacher training in English pedagogy is thus increasingly urgent.

2.1.2 Research on in-service teachers

MEXT also formulated an in-service teacher training system. First, MEXT trains leaders nationwide. The leaders train sub-leaders in their prefectures. The sub-leaders are to provide 30 hours of training to teachers in their schools. A survey conducted by a major educational organization in Japan (Benesse, 2010) asked 5,883 elementary school teachers who are in charge of 5th and 6th graders to answer a questionnaire. According to the survey, the responses to the question "How many hours did you take in-service training for English education at your school in 2009 and 2010?" are as follows: Only 5% of teachers had more than 25 hours of training; surprisingly, 20.4% of teachers had no training at all. As previously stated, MEXT requested the sub-leaders conduct 30 hours of teacher training at their schools over two years. Policies made at the top do not always get implemented at the bottom, especially if they do not involve the particular concerns of teachers (Fullan, 1991).

One of the reasons that teachers are reluctant to participate in training is that they are already overburdened with a heavy workload. Kusumoto (2008) revealed that 78.9% of elementary school teachers feel that conducting an English activity is a big burden, and nearly one-third of the participants think that English is not needed at the elementary school level. The survey by Benesse (2010) also revealed that 89.2% of teachers do not have enough time for preparing English lessons and 74.0% of teachers do not have enough time to talk with ALTs about lessons. That survey also revealed that 62.1% of teachers feel overloaded from teaching English. Elementary school teachers teach all subjects and do not have any planning time scheduled into their workday. This overload is a great concern for them.

2.1.3 Research on pre-service teachers

Kasuya et al. (2014) investigated students from Tokyo Gakugei University (a teacher education university). At this university, there are no required courses and only one elective course for teaching English in elementary schools; only a quarter of students take this course. According to Uchino (2015), there are teacher education universities that do not have any courses focused on teaching English at elementary schools, and even if there are, most of the courses are not compulsory. It is fair to say that many student teachers have not learned anything about teaching English at elementary schools before their graduation from a university. In addition, Kasuya et al. (2014) revealed that less than 30% of students had observed English lessons at an elementary school during their teaching practicums, and less than 10% of students had taught English during a teaching practicum. Students tend not to choose to teach English in their teaching practicums because elementary school pre-service teachers are not familiar with teaching English. Monoi (2013) pointed out that there are few opportunities to learn to teach English in a teaching practicum at elementary schools because of the lack of instructors who themselves can teach English. In the next section, I describe research on teachers' thinking.

2.2 Research on teachers' thinking in professional development

In this chapter, a brief literature review on particular areas of teacher development pertaining to this study is discussed. Teachers' thinking is important to research because it reveals the cognitive processes that influence teachers' actions. When conducting an exploratory study on teachers, we need to examine teachers' thinking.

2.2.1 Teachers' thinking

In previous literature on pedagogy, teachers' thinking has typically been ignored. Jackson's *Life in Classrooms* (1968) was a seminal study that looked at what teachers bring to the teaching process in terms of their mental constructs, a concept that was shelved by researchers in the positivist paradigm. The positivists investigate facts and causes. Consequently, research on thinking was thought to be too messy of a construct to control. Jackson had previously taken a quantitative, measurement-style approach to educational research, but he found something was missing. A measurement approach could not capture the messy realities of what goes on in classrooms. He then turned to ethnography and conducted qualitative research based on classroom observation. Jackson's early work set the stage for the research on teachers' thinking that would emerge in the 1980s.

Meanwhile, positivist-inspired research approaches, such as method comparison studies, indicated that paradigmatic change was needed. By the 1970s, because studies had reportedly failed to determine the best method, they were no longer carried out. In response to the failure of method comparison studies to come up with the best method, calls by educators emerged for studies more focused on teachers' thinking as they go through the process of teaching (Allwright, 1998). For example, Clark and Peterson (1986) conducted a critical study on teachers' thinking in general education. They proposed a model that points out the importance of including research on the mental domain of teaching in order to understand teaching behaviors in the classroom. Finally, around the 1990s, foreign language teacher education began to focus on the mental processes of teacher learning (Freeman, 1989; Gebhard, 1990; Gebhard & Oprandy, 1999; Johnson, 1999).

As pointed out above, it is doubtful that a "best method" can be developed that can be used by all teachers in any situations (Edge & Richards, 1998; Kumaravadivelu, 1994, 2001, 2003; McKeon, 1998). The complexities surrounding the classroom, including the differences in the way individual learners learn and individual teachers teach, make it difficult to support the idea of a standardized teaching method for all occasions. Over the last decade, the directionality of research in teacher learning has appeared to shift toward the mental aspects of teachers (e.g., beliefs, knowledge, decision making, etc.). In this approach, the goal is to learn more about why they do what they do in their instruction, rather than to provide prescriptive external accounts of what teachers should know (Freeman & Johnson, 1998). In the latter case, the teacher's mental constructs as manifested in their instruction are ignored, which then can only offer limited depictions of what goes on in the classroom.

To get a clearer picture of teaching in the classroom, according to Borg (2003), we need to view teachers as active, thinking decision makers who make instructional choices by drawing on complex, practically-oriented, personalized, and context-sensitive networks of knowledge, thoughts, and beliefs. He used the term "teacher cognition" and defined it as "what teachers think, know, and believe" (Borg, 2006, p. 1). Since Clandinin and Connelly (1987) noted that identical terms have been defined in different ways and different terms have been used to describe similar concepts, in this study, I use "teachers' thinking" as an inclusive term to embrace the complexity of teachers' mental lives. Historically speaking, research in this area has not been around long (Breen, Hird, Milton, Oliver, & Thwaite, 2001). Seventy-three percent of research studies on teachers' thinking in the field of second language learning was presented after 1996, and most of those studies examine English as a second language (ESL), not English as a foreign language (EFL) (Borg, 2003). Cowie (2011) noted a shortage of research on teachers' mental process in the EFL environment. Empirical research on the development of trainees' thinking during the process of taking a formal training program is limited (Borg, 2005). In most cases, researchers have concluded that teacher education focusing on teachers' thought processes did have an impact on participants' thinking (Borg, 2009). Teachers' thinking is key to investigating teacher development.

2.2.2 Teachers' beliefs

Teachers' beliefs are among the aspects of teachers' thinking that have been researched in regard to gaining a better understanding of why teachers do what they do in their instruction. Borg (2009, p. 381) reviewed teachers' beliefs as below. He wrote that teachers' beliefs:

- may be powerfully influenced (positively or negatively) by teachers' own experiences as learners and are well established by the time teachers go to university (Holt-Reynolds, 1992; Lortie, 1975);
- act as a filter through which teachers interpret new information and experiences (Pajares, 1992);
- may outweigh the effects of teacher education in influencing what teachers do in the classroom (Kagan, 1992; Richardson, 1996);
- can exert a persistent long-term influence on teachers' instructional practices (Crawley & Salyer, 1995);
- are, at the same time, not always reflected in what teachers do in the classroom (Dobson & Dobson, 1983; Pearson, 1985; Tabachnick & Zeichner, 1986);
- interact bi-directionally with experience (i.e., beliefs influence practices and practices can also lead to changes in beliefs) (Richardson, 1996).

From Borg's list, it is apparent that beliefs are a complex construct that is difficult to measure. However, this construct offers deep insights into teachers' thinking and for understanding why individual teachers do what they do. For example, images from prior experiences within formal language classrooms significantly affected teachers' images of themselves (Johnson, 1994). Teachers' beliefs play a role in motivating the actions of teachers in their practices and are powerful organizers in influencing teachers' decision-making, planning, and instruction.

2.2.3 Teacher autonomy

In recent years, teacher autonomy has emerged as a focus in the field of teacher education (Jiang & Ma, 2012). According to Smith (2003), common definitions of teacher autonomy have shifted from "a right to freedom from control" (Benson, 2000, p. 111) to teachers' capacity to engage in self-directed teaching (Little, 1995; Tort-Moloney, 1997) and to teachers' autonomy as learners (Smith, 2000). There is interaction within an individual between autonomy as a language learner and autonomy as a language teacher (Huang, 2007). Little (1995) gave rise to the concept of "teacher-learner autonomy." The term was then used by Smith (2003), by which he meant that teachers are learners in a variety of areas, including pedagogical skills and knowledge, languages, etc. Smith (2003) defined the concept as the ability to develop appropriate skills, knowledge, and attitudes for oneself as a teacher, in cooperation with others.

2.2.4 Research on in-service teachers' thinking

MEXT states an HRT's roles in an English lesson as follows:

> The instructors must formulate topics and activities through which pupils will be motivated to convey their thoughts to others and learn more about others. HRTs are able to do this since they know the interests and daily lives of their pupils and the kind of knowledge and skills their pupils have acquired in other subjects. Even if they do not speak English fluently, their positive attitude toward interaction through English will serve as an extremely important catalyst to enhance pupils' interest in foreign languages. Thus, HRTs are indispensable in Foreign Language Activities. (Gifu JETs, 2010, p. 10)

Although MEXT does not include the expectation that they speak English fluently, the emphasis on communication in English is nonetheless challenging for elementary school teachers. According to Benesse (2010), more than two-thirds (68.1%) of elementary school teachers said they do not have self-confidence in teaching English. Current teachers were not required to take any coursework related to teaching English while studying for the teacher certificate in college (Machida, 2016). The next question regards the level of English competence needed to teach English. Again, more than two-thirds (68.0%) of teachers felt that they do not have enough English competence.

S. Matsumiya (2013) investigated elementary school teachers' anxiety. The results of that study showed that they experienced anxiety related to their English competence, which in turn caused anxiety about teaching English. Shinato (2012) interviewed three elementary school teachers using a qualitative approach and found that, although they felt anxious, they had become familiar with teaching English. The reported results above indicate that teachers experience anxiety. Responding to the recent drastic change in English education at the elementary school level in Japan, HRTs' needs should be investigated (Kusumoto, 2008). Voices from critical stakeholders need to be taken into consideration in the process of policy implementation (Nagamine, 2012). If teachers do not see themselves as stakeholders in curriculum policy reform, they may be reluctant to change.

2.2.5 Research on pre-service teachers' thinking

There have been several studies conducted on pre-service teachers' thinking. Nahatame (2014) found that they experienced anxiety about their speaking, especially their pronunciation of English, and they needed opportunities to observe and conduct lessons. Monoi (2013) conducted a survey with university students and the results indicated that students could gain knowledge regarding teaching English depending on the curriculum offered by their universities, but that their anxiety may be difficult to alleviate in a short amount of time. N. Matsumiya (2013) attempted to use speech practice to foster university students' English proficiency in order to ease their anxiety, and the results revealed that many of the participants found the practice enjoyable and effective; however, many of them were still anxious about their English abilities. Tanaka, Honda, Osada, and Nishi (2013) investigated the thinking of pre-service teachers who attended their teacher training program by conducting a survey. The results indicated that pre-service teachers thought they needed English competence and instructional skills. English proficiency seems to be of great concern for pre-service teachers.

There is little research about pre-service teachers' teaching practicums focusing specifically on teaching English (Tanaka et al., 2013). Itoi (2014) revealed that pre-service teachers realized during their teaching practicums that their English was not proficient enough. There has still been little research that focuses on the developmental process of pre-service teachers regarding teaching English during their teaching practicums. Thus, in this study, I would like to describe how pre-service teachers develop during their teaching practicums. In the next section, I describe lesson study.

2.3 Research on lesson study

In this section, I describe what lesson study is and its significance for teacher development.

2.3.1 Lesson study

Lesson study has a long history. The origins of lesson study can be traced back to the 1920s. According to the National Association for the Study of Education Methods (2011), lesson study originated in Japan and is spreading internationally. The term *lesson study* is a direct translation of the two Japanese words *jugyo* and *kenkyu*, which mean lesson and study, respectively (Fernandez & Yoshida, 2004). It is the most common form of professional teacher development in Japan (Lewis, 2000; Lewis & Tsuchida, 1998; Murata & Takahashi, 2002; Takahashi, 2000; Takahashi & Yoshida, 2004; Yoshida, 1999). The average Japanese teacher sees or conducts lesson study about ten times per year (Yoshida, 1999). Lesson study in Japan is generally conducted in elementary schools. In elementary schools, teachers have common interests and experiences because they are all capable of teaching any subject at any grade level. In other words, these teachers already have similar problems and backgrounds that enable them to have collaborative and collegial relationships. Various forms of lesson study exist, including district- and national-level lesson study (Murata & Takahashi, 2002; Takahashi, 2006). Among them, school-based lesson study with the involvement of the entire faculty is the most common. The percentage of Japanese elementary schools that conduct school-based lesson study is 99.3 (*Kokuritsu-kyoiku-seisaku-kenkyusho* [National Education Policy Research Institute], 2011). Japanese teachers traditionally collaborate with each other within one school. Researchers who describe one cycle of lesson study tend to underemphasize the fact that Japanese school-based lesson study is an ongoing part of an academic year and is conducted school-wide. In Japan, teachers in one school set a research theme at the start of the academic year, as well as a schedule of implementation for lesson study cycles.

In a lesson study cycle, one teacher who takes charge in a research lesson makes a draft of a lesson plan. Then all members examine the draft from various points of view and exchange their ideas and experiences in order to carry out what is called polishing or smoothing out of any rough spots of the lesson plan. During a research lesson, one teacher conducts a lesson while others observe and collect data using an evaluation sheet. Finally, in the post-lesson discussion, all members discuss the good practices, the tasks to be improved, and the proposal of possible ideas by using the data noted on their evaluation sheets. Schools usually invite a university professor or a supervisor from the school board as a more knowledgeable other (MKO), which refers to someone who has a better understanding or a higher ability level than the learner (learner, in this case, refers to teachers), following Vygotsky's theory (Moll, 1990). "Lesson study is a process in which teachers jointly plan, observe, analyze, and refine actual classroom lessons called research lessons" (Burghes & Robinson, 2009, p. 7). Figure 2.1 shows a lesson study cycle.

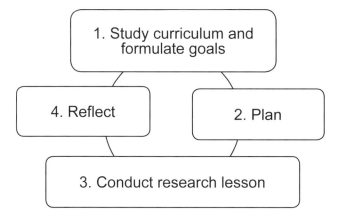

Figure 2.1. Lesson study cycle including studying curriculum and formulating goals, planning, conducting a research lesson, and reflecting (Redrawn from Lewis & Hurd, 2011, p. 2)

MEXT stated that the following are the objectives of school-based lesson study:

1. To improve the teaching abilities of each teacher and maintain or improve the school's standard of teacher quality.
2. To enhance mutual understanding among teachers, and have them share a common goal for improving their teaching abilities.
3. All teachers share their concerns, problems and challenges through observing pupils during other teachers' lessons.
4. Improve the teaching skills of each teacher by learning, through actual observation of lessons, excellent teaching methods and techniques for developing teaching materials. (Gifu JETs, 2010, p. 124)

MEXT refers not only to the teaching abilities of each teacher, but also to the school's standard of teacher quality and the mutual understanding among teachers. School-based lesson study has an important role in Japan in terms of building human relations within a school and drawing everyone into a shared school-wide research theme that they all care about. This helps build a sense of collective responsibility for students.

The competence and quality appropriate to the professional responsibility of teachers are developed gradually, and the professional development of teachers is a lifelong process. Common misconceptions internationally are that lesson study improves instruction primarily through improved lesson plans, that lesson study produces a library of perfect lessons, and that the research lesson is a demonstration lesson or an expert lesson (Lewis, 2002). In fact, U.S. lesson study groups work together on an ad hoc basis, without a long-term expectation of continued work together. However, lesson study does not only improve lesson plans. More importantly, it is focused on making the classroom a place where professional conversations about teaching and learning occur (Takahashi & Yoshida, 2004). Lesson study is not just for initial teacher training but also for career development.

Lesson study in Japan has also been conducted as part of pre-service teacher development. Fernandez (2002) reported that pre-service teachers in Japan frequently conduct lesson study as part of their teaching practicums:

> They will prepare a study lesson in collaboration with their university-based mentors and the teacher with whom they have been assigned to work at their school site. They will then teach the lesson in this school, and all the teachers in the building, the university mentors, and other student teachers will come observe. (p. 395)

Stigler and Hiebert (1999) discussed pre-service teacher development in the U.S.:

> Lesson study is a new concept for teachers entering the profession. If undergraduate methods courses were restructured to introduce students to collaboratively planning and testing lessons, new teachers would be ready to assume leadership roles more quickly. (p. 158)

Lesson study is rarely conducted for pre-service teachers in the U.S.

2.3.2 The international spread of lesson study

Lesson study was introduced in *The Teaching Gap* by Stigler and Hiebert (1999) in the U.S. and has since spread internationally. In 2006, the World Association of Lesson Studies (WALS) was established. Xu and Pedder (2015) identified 67 articles published between 2002 and 2013. Most of these articles, with the exception of two, were published by researchers outside Japan. Between 2002 and 2007, 17 articles were published. Between 2008 and 2013, number leapt to 50 articles published. Forty-nine articles focused on the benefits and constraints that influence lesson study in different contexts. Twenty-one studies highlighted the benefits of teacher collaboration through lesson study. "These studies reported an increase in teachers' collegiality, joint decision making, and joint ownership and responsibility for teaching leading to the cultivation of learning communities" (Xu & Pedder, 2015, p. 38). The most frequently mentioned constraints are the lack of time and the lack of strong leadership. Stigler and Hiebert (1999) noted that local adaptations and variations of lesson study are only to be expected. Several researchers have explicitly outlined the framework of lesson study and how it should be introduced and have provided examples of lesson study projects in the U.S. (Lewis, Perry, & Murata, 2006).

2.3.3 Lesson study as teacher collaboration

The core principle of lesson study is teacher collaboration. Lesson study promotes teachers' collaboration in an effort to improve teaching and learning in schools (Stigler & Hiebert, 1999). Unlike one-size-fits-all, pushed-in, or top-down approaches to professional development, lesson study allows teachers to bring their own questions to the table (Lewis & Hurd, 2011). Thus, lesson study is a collaborative teacher development system that is ingrained in the school culture of Japan.

On the other hand, in the U.S., because there is no consistent culture of teacher collaboration in schools, if teachers want to do lesson study, they have to organize it themselves. The teaching culture in North America becomes isolating over time because the majority of teachers spend their days in their own classrooms, often with the door closed (Stigler & Hiebert, 1999). Lesson study is not officially supported or organized institutionally by departments of education or school boards. Teachers must recruit group members and start lesson study on their own. In the U.S., the role of teacher collaboration in lesson study is considered to be one of the most valued aspects.

Lesson study builds collaboration as teachers progressively improve lessons that are "our" lessons, rather than "my" lessons (Lewis & Hurd, 2011, p. 3). A short-term and pre-packaged program is organized without consideration of teachers' specific needs and problems or the realities of their classrooms (Triwaranyu, 2007). Lewis and Hurd (2011) compared lesson study and traditional teacher development, citing Liptak (2005). Table 2.1 presents the construction of these two views of professional development. As it shows, lesson study places teachers in an active role as researchers.

Table 2.1

Comparison of Lesson Study and Traditional Teacher Development (Redrawn from Lewis & Hurd, 2011, p. 7)

TRADITIONAL	LESSON STUDY
Begins with answer	Begins with question
Driven by outside "expert"	Driven by participants
Communication flow: trainer → teachers	Communication flow: among teachers
Hierarchical relations between trainer and learners	Reciprocal relations among learners
Research informs practice	Practice is research

The collaborative nature of the lesson study process values the rich experience teachers have and provides opportunities for them to share their knowledge stemming from classroom practices. Lesson study changes school culture and teachers develop a common language (Lewis & Hurd, 2011). Knowledge sharing in collaboration is dialectical (Burroughs & Luebeck, 2010). Teachers can provide differing views or insights from this interaction, and new information or knowledge emerges.

2.3.4 Lesson study and reflection

In the 1930s, John Dewy defined the term *reflection* as active, persistent, and careful consideration of any belief or supposed form of knowledge (Richards & Ho, 1998). Schön (1983, 1987) argued that reflection is inextricably bound to action. Rather than attempting to apply scientific theories and concepts to practical situations, he held that professionals should learn to frame and reframe the often complex and ambiguous problems they are facing, test out various interpretations, and then modify their actions as a result (Hatton & Smith, 1995). In sum, reflection involves teachers in thinking about their work, understanding what they and their learners do, and considering ways of improving the quality of teaching and learning (A'Dhahab, 2009). Therefore, reflection is considered to be a key concept in teacher development.

Research on teacher education in the 1980s and 1990s shifted the paradigm from the traditional skill-based orientation of "teacher's training" to a more cognitive analysis, "teacher development" (Hatta, 1996). This shift has led to more research attention on teachers' thought processes, what teachers themselves think and know, and how they "make sense of or interpret classroom scenes" (Carter & Doyle, 1987, p. 148). In the early 1980s, reflection received much interest in the education research community. Reflection is now increasingly recognized as playing an important role in teacher professional development. Although few opportunities have been provided to very busy teachers, reflection is conducted with peers in lesson study (Sasajime, 2009). Reflection promotes teachers' lifelong professional development, and constant reflection plays a critical role in empowering teachers (Nagamine, 2011). By being reflective, teachers are expected to gain awareness of their own teaching beliefs and practices, allowing them to see teaching differently (Fanselow, 1988; Gebhard & Oprandy, 1999).

2.3.5 Lesson study and action research

Lesson study is similar to action research, which is the study of a social situation involving the participants themselves as researchers, with a view toward improving the quality of the action within it (Somekh, 1989). Kurt Lewin promoted action research in the 1930s. He used a spiral of steps, each of which is composed of a circle of planning, action, and fact-finding regarding the result of the action (Burns, 1999). This approach has been utilized in a wide range of areas, such as sociology, psychology, and pedagogy. The idea of action research was taken up vigorously in the education field in the 1950s, but later went into decline. It came under criticism during the 1960s when positivistic, scientific approaches to research were dominant. In the 1970s it received a new impetus in the U.K. Elliott, for example, further developed action research as a form of professional development for teachers (Nasrollahi, Krish, & Noor, 2012).

Both action research and lesson study models involve teachers doing research on their own classes in a look, think, do, reflect, and revise approach. Both involve teachers as researchers in their classrooms. Classrooms are complex environments where teachers are concerned with the particularities of their students' needs, course aims, and meeting particular goals of the local school they teach in. It is hard to suggest a standardized approach to teacher development. It is unrealistic to suggest a quality all-purpose teaching model for teachers to follow. Under the complex circumstances presented by classrooms, teachers themselves are in the best position to identify problems concerning their particular situations and to discover ways to solve them (Laskowski, 2009).

The approaches of action research and lesson study are similar because teachers conduct research on their own classes, and they do so in a similar, systematic way (Laskowski, 2009). However, a main difference is that lesson study in Japan is usually implemented within a school as a school-based professional development program (Yoshida, 1999), which is fully supported and sometimes required by the local school board. In the case of action research, teachers can begin research when they identify problems, and finish it when they solve those problems. On the other hand, in school-based lesson study, one school year is considered one cycle. Teachers at the school should be included in lesson study. The core principle of lesson study is school-based teacher collaboration.

2.3.6 The need for more research documented in Japan

Although lesson study is spreading internationally, there are very few published studies in English on lesson study conducted in Japan. Stingler and Hiebert (1999) stated that "very little has been written in English about the process of lesson study" (p. 111). Laskowski (2011) also wrote that

> there are a number of published papers and books on lesson study written by researchers and teachers in America. On the other hand, there has not been much of a need to describe the procedures and merits of lesson study in Japanese literature on education because it is the most common form of teacher development and therefore implicitly understood. (p. 74)

Ermeling and Graff-Ermeling (2014) pointed out the following:

> Despite the growing popularity of lesson study and increasing volume of publications, the descriptive knowledge base of lesson study in Japan is still limited to a few fully developed Japanese cases. These are currently no published first-person accounts of lesson study in Japan. Expanding the descriptive knowledge base with more examples from Japan remains an important priority to increase our understanding of authentic lesson study. (p. 172)

Lewis, Perry, and Murata (2006) also called for more Japan examples to better understand the features of lesson study in its native context. Pre-service teacher development is in the same situation. Few publications have provided descriptions of how to include pre-service teachers in lesson study (Fernandez,

2002; Hiebert, Morris, & Glass, 2003, Post & Varoz, 2008). Thus, I introduce the chosen case in order to describe a narrative of lesson study in Japan in English. One of the purposes of this study is to contribute to the expansion of descriptive cases on lesson study.

2.3.7 Recent problem with lesson study in Japan

Despite being evaluated at the international level, lesson study in Japan has become just routine work as in-service teachers' professional development (Inagaki & Sato, 1996). Murase (2007) also stated that lesson study as in-school development has resulted in superficiality, becoming routine work that sets limited objectives; the problem is that no part of it contributes to the development of teaching. Sasajima and Borg (2009) pointed out that lesson study in Japan tends to become a show-like performance of a perfect lesson. It is not like the real classrooms of most teachers. He suggested that lesson study should focus on teachers' thinking. In addition, giving way to older or more experienced teachers causes limitations in collaborative dialog in Japan. For example, Fletcher (2005) wrote:

> The culture of waiting for a party of experts to pronounce on the merits and weaknesses of a lesson rather than engaging in democratic debate may be an opportunity as yet not fully exploited for the growth of new knowledge about pedagogy. (p. 2)

Japan is usually associated with a hierarchical apprenticeship model.

Lesson study is the most common form of teacher development in Japan. It has been handed down to teachers for years and risks devolving into a superficial endeavor. Japanese educators need to remember the effectiveness of lesson study and realize its value for collaboration.

2.3.8 Research on lesson study pertaining to teaching English in elementary schools

Although school-based lesson study is one of the major professional development components used in Japan, there are few studies on school-based lesson study for teaching English in elementary schools. Tsuji (2010) participated in school-based lesson study and identified the following factors: model class exhibition, observation classes, post-lesson discussions, experiencing the activity contents, and learning about theory. Nakayama (2011, 2012) researched the effects of school-based lesson study on teachers. The results indicated that teachers were affected by children's growth patterns, colleague's cooperation, understanding of English lessons' communication principles, and pleasure in English lessons. I believe there needs to be more research on school-based lesson study as it pertains to teaching English in elementary schools.

2.4 Methodological perspectives and paradigms

In this section, I describe methodological perspectives and paradigms.

2.4.1 Perspectives and paradigms

Research is based on paradigms, mainly the positivist or the interpretivist (Punch, 1998). Neuman (1991) defined a paradigm as "a framework or a set of assumptions that explain how the world is perceived" (p. 57). He distinguished between positivism and interpretivism paradigms. Khan (2014) explained Neuman's definition as such: "The positivist view of the world is objective where behaviour and cause and effect can be measured and human activity can be predicted" (p. 225). This means that results can be generalized, as a large number of participants can participate in the research. On the other hand, he explained an interpretivist view as follows:

> An interpretivist view of the world is subjective, where individuals form their own reality of the world in different contexts through interactions with others. Every individual perceives the world differently and views it in different contexts. Therefore, their actions and behaviours are unpredictable. (p. 225)

This suggests that the results are not generalized, but instead are grounded in the particular realities of each participant and provide in-depth accounts of the subjects.

These paradigms are based on two perspectives: ontology and epistemology (Denzin & Lincoln, 2003; Punch, 2013). Ontology is concerned with the nature of reality (Creswell, 2007; Punch, 1998), while epistemology is concerned with the researchers' perception of reality (Creswell, 2007; Gratton & Jones, 2004; Punch, 1998).

This study is based upon epistemology and an interpretivist approach, which implies that the researcher attempts to see the world from the participants' perspectives and considers their perceptions. Denzin and Lincoln (2003) explained that this is because an interpretivist approach depends on both the participant's *emic* (intrinsic, how local people think) view and the researcher's *etic* (extrinsic, generalizations about human behavior) view. That is to say, the researcher can find meaning in a participant's action. The interpretivist approach, with the inclusion of the emic and etic roles in collecting and analyzing data, allows the researcher to theorize about the data, and at the same time to substantiate theories expressed in data taken from participants (Watson-Gegeo, 1988).

2.4.2 Taking a qualitative approach

There are two standard ways of conducting research: the quantitative approach and the qualitative approach. A quantitative approach is experimental, focuses on numerical data, and uses statistical analysis. It is used to generalize results from a larger sample population. Quantitative data collection methods include various forms of surveys. A qualitative approach, on the other hand, is an interpretive and naturalistic approach and is non-experimental, focusing on verbal narratives like spoken or written data. A qualitative research design provides the best means to explore complex processes and investigate little-known phenomena. As Denzin and Lincoln (1994) wrote, "Qualitative researchers study things in their natural settings, attempting to make sense of, or interpret phenomena in terms of the meanings people bring to them" (p. 2). Therefore, subjectivity is valued. Consequently, a qualitative approach allows the researcher to get closer to the data to conduct an in-depth analysis of the subjects and typically requires a smaller sample size than quantitative analyses. This study uses a qualitative approach. It is non-experimental, uses qualitative data (interviews, video recordings of discussions, etc.), and applies an interpretative analysis to understand elementary school teachers' thinking about teaching English.

2.4.3 Grounded theory approach (GTA)

Glaser and Strauss' (1967) grounded theory approach (GTA) comprises a discovery-oriented research framework aimed at gaining insights from the point of view of participants. It is a way of strengthening qualitative research.

GTA is an inductive approach through which theory is generated from the data, rather than an approach in which the researcher is testing a preconceived idea or hypothesis (Strauss & Corbin, 1998). In sociology, GTA was conceived to bridge the gap between theory and empirical research by connecting theory to evidence through the process of engaging with the data rather than using a deductive approach (Dey, 2004).

Glaser and Strauss (1967), the originators of GTA, used the *constant comparative* method of analysis. This process is reiterative, as data collection and analysis occur almost simultaneously. The idea is that a researcher gathers and analyzes data, and then compares them with previously collected data in order to determine variables. In GTA, sampling is conducted according to the principle of *theoretical sampling*. As the data are collected and analyzed, it is continually decided on the spot what data are to be collected next (Glaser & Strauss, 1967; Strauss & Corbin, 1998). The concept of *theoretical saturation* (when data collections cease to offer new understandings) is relied on to achieve an appropriate sample size in qualitative studies. However, Thompson (2011) pointed out that little has been written about sample size. Following Glaser and Strauss, Thompson (2011) also stated that sample size should be determined by the point of *theoretical saturation,* which can be affected by the scope of the research question, the sensitivity of the phenomena, and the ability of the researcher. Patton (1990) wrote that when deciding on sample size, there is no precise number. He posited that the number depends on the purpose of the research, what the researchers hope to learn, and the feasibility of accomplishing what the researchers wish to achieve within a reasonable time-frame with the resources available.

Since Glaser and Strauss first developed GTA in 1967, it has continued to evolve through a developmental process of amendments over the last five decades, as they specified very little in the way of coding (Suddaby, 2006). Moreover, a rift emerged between the two founders after each altered their method in different ways. GTA is thus split into two main versions: the Glaser version (Glaser, 1978, 1992) and the Strauss and Corbin version (Strauss, 1987; Strauss & Corbin, 1990, 1998).

These versions reflect the different philosophical backgrounds of the two founders. According to Charmaz (2006), Glaser's background lies in Columbia University positivism, while Strauss was educated at the Chicago School of Sociology, with its stress on qualitative research. At first, Glaser (1992) specified phases to analyze the data: *open coding, selective coding,* and *theoretical coding.* He suggested 18 coding families, covering ideas like dimensions and elements, mutual effects and reciprocity, social control, recruitment and isolation, and many other ideas for categories and relationships. Glaser (2005) has since introduced 23 new coding families, expanding the number of coding families to 41 in total. However, these are difficult to understand, especially for novice researchers. On the other hand, Strauss (1987) moved the method toward verification, and Strauss and Corbin's GTA version is better-known than the earlier version (Khan, 2014) because its detailed and systematic methods are friendlier for the novice user. Strauss and Corbin (1990, 1998) elaborated on the original work and divided the data analysis process into three main phases, *open coding, axial coding,* and *selective coding,* which are the most widely accepted in the world.

In Strauss and Corbin's (1998) version, the data are transcribed verbatim. Every word, phrase, or sentence in each line of data is analyzed. Each analyzed line is then broken down into codes. This microscopic analysis serves to prevent researchers from biased analyses. Then, during *open coding,* the codes are compared, and similar codes are grouped together, with each group becoming a concept. These concepts are contrasted and clustered on an abstract level as categories (Strauss & Corbin, 1998). *Axial coding* is the "process of relating categories to their subcategories" (Strauss & Corbin, 1998, p. 123). In other words, axial coding comprises "intense analysis around one category" (Strauss, 1987, p. 32) using properties and dimensions. Properties ask "What are the characteristics of items?" or "What attributes are specific to this one concept?" Dimensions answer questions about the variance of such properties (Strauss & Corbin, 1998). LaRossa (2005) wrote that there is confusion about the mechanics of axial coding:

> Strauss and Corbin's (1990, 1998) use of the term *subcategory* is not very helpful. In many people's minds, the prefix *sub* denotes under or beneath as in submarine or subsample. Thus, a subcategory can be thought to refer to a category that is under another category (e.g., pens and pencils subsumed under writing instruments). But this is not how sub has been used in Strauss and Corbin's version of GTM [grounded theory methods]. In their scheme, subcategory denotes a category that is related to-not a subclass of-a focal category. (pp. 847-848)

Saiki (2014), a student of Strauss, also noted misunderstanding of the term "subcategory." After one primary category is chosen from among various categories, the other categories then become subcategories; that is, they become related categories that further inform the selected category. According to Strauss and Corbin (1998), "subcategories answer questions about the phenomenon such as when, where, why, who, how, and with what consequences" (p. 125). *Selective coding* leads to the formation of core themes that operate as an umbrella category (or categories) with which to cover the data labeled under open and axial coding. Thus, "selective coding refers to the integration of the categories to structure the initial theoretical framework so as to analytically come up with the grounded theory from the data" (Khiat, 2010, p. 1472). This continues until *theoretical saturation* has been reached; that is, when data collections offers no new understandings (Strauss & Corbin, 1990). Strauss and Corbin (1998) stated that this process is "a free-flowing and creative one in which analysts move quickly back and forth between types of coding, using analytic techniques and procedures freely" (p. 58).

Glaser, however, did not agree with the concept of *axial coding*. He thought that it would encourage researchers to force conceptual linkages upon their data. "In his view, the stage of *axial coding* is too rigid, forces data, hinders emergence and leads to conceptual description instead of grounded theory" (Seidel & Urquhart, 2013, p. 237). Glaser noted that conceptual linkages between or among variables should emerge without bias from the researcher. Glaser (1992) also strongly argued that research should begin in an area of interest to understand a phenomenon with no preliminary literature review and no defined research problem prior to the first interviews and observations. The initial data collections should help the researcher discover the "emergent" research problem (Glaser, 1992). Strauss, on the other hand, moved toward favoring the selection of a research problem before beginning a research project (Strauss & Corbin, 1998). Whereas Glaser placed a heavy emphasis on the unbiased view of emergence, Strauss and Corbin adopted the view that a researcher does play a role in emergence and that this reality should be taken into consideration. Strauss argued that it is naïve to assume that a researcher with an educational background could enter a research situation, as Glaser believed, with a *tabula rasa* (i.e., without any preconceived views of the research environment). Adopting their view, it would be unrealistic to assume that researchers could enter into that environment with no preconceptions.

2.5 Summary of chapter

In this chapter, the discussion focused on teaching English in elementary schools and teachers' thinking as critical factors in teacher development. Next, lesson study in Japan was reviewed as an appropriate framework to involve teachers in their own development. Finally, methodological perspectives and paradigms were reviewed. In sum, this study is different from previous studies because it:

- focuses on elementary school in-service teachers who have not had any experience or training in teaching English.
- investigates pre-service teachers during their teaching practicums
- interprets teachers' thinking using a qualitative approach
- describes lesson study conducted in Japan in English.

The methodological procedures used in this study that are directly related to both a qualitative approach and GTA are addressed in the next chapter.

Chapter 3

Methodology

In this chapter, the methodology applied in this study is presented. First, I describe the M-GTA that was selected for this study. Second, the validity and reliability of my methodology are described.

3.1 Modified grounded theory approach (M-GTA)

M-GTA is a modified version of GTA that was developed by Kinoshita (2003, 2007). Kinoshita (2003) wrote that all versions of GTA should have the following five components: 1) They should be grounded in data, from which a theory is generated, 2) data are categorized using *open coding* and *selective coding*, 3) categories emerge from data using the *constant comparative* method, 4) *theoretical sampling* occurs as the researcher considers the next steps in data collection, and 5) *theoretical saturation* should be reached, in which conceptual categories have sufficient, substantial evidence to support them.

Kinoshita (2003) recognized that Glaser, who was trained in quantitative methodology, aimed at rigorous analysis (e.g., data were broken down minutely into words, phrases, or utterances and were labeled by categorizing them into codes) for qualitative studies to protest against the preoccupation of quantitative studies. Kinoshita (2003) understood that this would be meaningful because qualitative approaches suffered from being labeled as impressionistic and criticized for not being rigorous or systematic; on the other hand, in the 1960s, quantitative methods were seen as rigorous and scientific.

However, Kinoshita deviated from Glaser's approach in two distinct ways. One is the researcher's role in the emergence of the data, and the other is the fragmentation of data during the coding process. He disagreed with Glaser's insistence on the "emergence from data," unbiased from the researcher, finding it unrealistic (Kinoshita, 2003). Kinoshita (2003) was in agreement with Strauss on this point. He evaluated Strauss as an interactionist and an interpretivist, and followed his stance that the researcher plays an interactive role in categorical formation from the data. However, Kinoshita (2003) disagreed with Strauss's position that data should be broken down into small chunks, labeled, and coded. He insisted that fine fragmentation narrows the context of participants' statements or actions, which would otherwise help researchers to formulate richer concepts from the data.

In relation to the above, M-GTA differs from GTA in terms of its strict coding procedures. It does not employ the method of finely fragmenting the data (e.g., coding the data line by line, etc.), and it forms concepts directly from interpretations of data on an analysis worksheet, not using codes (Kinoshita, 2003). Analyzing codes in the second and third stages of analysis in GTA makes interpretation difficult (Kinoshita, 2003). Although the data have been fragmented for rigid analysis, researchers cannot be unbiased and transparent. They need questions and interest to analyze data. In M-GTA, researchers conduct a preliminary literature review and define a research problem before conducting interviews. It is necessary that the researcher have his/her own view or theoretical stance on his/her own research. Saiki (2014) analyzed 430 Japanese articles that utilized grounded theory. The findings indicate that

M-GTA was adopted in 213 articles. Thus, it can be said that M-GTA is well known in Japan.

M-GTA is adopted in this study because understanding the particular context in which the participants operate is important in order to derive the mental processes. M-GTA is an analysis method suitable for cases with process characteristics, such as when research subjects change throughout a process. Additionally, M-GTA is suitable for analyzing interview data and focuses on organizing substantive theory for practical utilization (Kinoshita, 1999, 2003).

3.2 Analysis procedure of M-GTA

M-GTA aims to generate knowledge that can be generalized within a limited and particular scope. It requires the following condition-setting using the terminology put forth by Kinoshita (2003): the *Researcher-At-Work* generates the knowledge through the *Analytically-Focused Person*, and the individuals apply the knowledge in actual settings through the viewpoints of the *Analytically-Focused Person*. In this study, *Researcher-At-Work* is a researcher who would like to know the developmental process of elementary school teachers associated with teaching English. *Analytically-Focused Person* (collective others, standard for the selection of subjects) are elementary school in-service and pre-service teachers who conduct lesson study. The actual people who cooperated in this study are described as participants in each chapter (see Chapters 4 & 6). M-GTA requires that *Analytical Themes* be clarified, meaning research questions need to be composed. Three research questions are posed in this study (see Chapter 1).

The analysis was conducted in the following manner. To avoid fragmentation of the data analysis, M-GTA used a two-stage procedure. *Open coding* comprised concept formation, while *selective coding* comprised thematic category formation. During *open coding,* all written responses or recorded interviews and discussions were transcribed verbatim. Sentences that seemed to have similar patterns were gathered and given a concept name. Analysis worksheets were then created. Kinoshita (2003) recommended using word processing software rather than spreadsheet software. On an analysis worksheet (see Appendices 1, 4, & 7), a concept name, its definition, examples, and theoretical notes were recorded. Questions, ideas, opposite examples, etc., were recorded in theoretical notes. One analysis worksheet was created for each concept (Okazaki, 2012). In *selective coding,* several concepts were integrated into a category and several categories were integrated into a core-category. Core-categories are not always necessary in M-GTA (Kinoshita, 2003). A diagram with descriptions of the relationships among concepts, categories, and core-categories was developed according to the results. Then, the storyline, which is a narrative theme with the words of concepts, categories, and core-categories, was presented. To further clarify the analytical process of M-GTA taken in this study, the following steps are shown:

1. The data taken from participants was transcribed.
2. The transcripts were analyzed to search for concepts.
3. After locating data that substantially supported a concept, an analysis worksheet was made. (Open coding)
4. Core-categories and categories to conceptualize the concepts were formed. (Selective coding)
5. Thematic relationships showing interconnectivity of concepts, categories, and core-categories were presented in a diagram.
6. The storyline, which forms conceptualizations to explain the results of the analysis of the concepts, categories, and core-categories, was written.

In a *constant comparative* method, data are gathered, analyzed, and compared against previously collected data. Regarding *theoretical sampling* (purposeful sampling), Kinoshita (2003) used "methodological restriction," which means that sampling should be restricted to the research questions. He stated that the sample size may best be determined by the study objectives. The point of *theoretical saturation* should be determined by the scope of the research question and the practicality of time allotment, as well as the availability of appropriate resources to conduct the study. Kinoshita (2003) mentioned that regarding the decision of when *theoretical saturation* has been reached, it is difficult to determine precisely where the cutoff point should be in the data collection and analysis process, and that this does not have to be done perfectly.

3.3 Validity and reliability

In quantitative research, validity refers to the believability of the research. There are two aspects of validity. Internal validity comprises the appropriateness of the instruments or procedures used in the research. External validity means that the results can be generalized beyond the immediate study. Reliability refers to the replication of findings (Merriam, 1998).

Since validity and reliability are rooted in positivist perspectives, they must be refined for use in an interpretivist approach (Golafshani, 2003). Lincoln and Guba (1985) proposed rigorous criteria for judging qualitative research and explicitly offered them as an alternative to quantitative criteria. "Credibility" is an alternative to internal validity. It denotes that the results of qualitative research are credible or believable from the participants' perspectives. Longitudinal observation of participants, triangulation, and peer debriefing are needed to show "credibility." "Transferability" is an alternative to external validity and refers to the degree to which the results of qualitative research can be transferred to or resonate with other contexts or settings. This requires a thorough description of the research process. In qualitative research, there is no expectation of replication (Simon, 2011), as the in-depth analysis of a phenomenon within the particular context in which it exists may be difficult to replicate. The essence of reliability for qualitative research lies in the consistency of the data and results (Leung, 2015). Lincoln and Guba (1985) used the term "dependability" in qualitative research, which closely corresponds to the notion of reliability in quantitative research. It is necessary to document all procedures in the study to increase the consistency (Creswell, 2009). Thick description, which comprises a detailed account of the context and a description of the procedures from beginning to end, allows readers to follow the process and understand validity and reliability in the study.

There are various approaches a researcher can take to address validity and reliability in qualitative studies. The most popular of these are triangulation and peer debriefing (Simon, 2011). "Triangulation is the process of corroborating evidence from different individuals, types of data, or methods of data collection" (Creswell, 2005, p. 600). In this study, data were collected from five pre-service teachers and six in-service teachers (different individuals). Video recordings of the pre-service and in-service teachers' discussions, an open-ended questionnaire and follow up interviews, the pre-service teachers' logs, video recordings of the teachers' lessons, lesson plans, proceedings from all meetings, a booklet published in the school, and my field notes were all collected for triangulated data to show qualitative rigor (different types of data or methods of data collection). "Peer debriefing is the review of the data and research process by someone who is familiar with the research or the phenomenon being explored"

(Creswell & Miller, 2000, p. 129). Peer debriefing requires researchers to work together with one or several colleagues who hold impartial views on the study. The impartial peers examine the researcher's transcripts, final report, and general methodology. Afterward, feedback is provided to ensure validity and reliability. In this study, I chose my co-worker whose major is Japanese education and who has experience using M-GTA. I explained the purpose of this study and the participants derived from *theoretical sampling* (purposeful sampling) and asked her to develop concepts from the transcripts. Some of her concepts were different from mine, so we discussed which were better. I also showed the peer reviewer the diagram and storyline, and got feedback from her. The process of peer debriefing is written in each chapter (Chapters 4 & 6) in detail. Member check, the process of showing participants the emerged concepts and categories and obtaining feedback, is not necessary in M-GTA (Kinoshita, 2003).

In sorting out the data, text mining is one way to conduct a micro-analysis of text. Although context plays a major role in M-GTA, limiting the use of text mining software, I used KH Coder Ver.2 to determine frequent words and co-occurrence networks to make sure that important words were not missed.

3.4 Summary of chapter

In this chapter, the methodology for this study was described. First, I described the M-GTA that was selected for this study. Second, validity and reliability were described. Triangulation, peer debriefing, and thick description of the analysis process help readers understand validity and reliability. Detailed data collection and analysis are presented in Chapter 4 and Chapter 6.

Chapter 4

Study on pre-service teachers

Pre-service teachers' practicums for teaching English are uncommon (see Chapter 2, section 2.1.3). In this chapter, based on the data, an analysis of how pre-service teachers developed regarding teaching English during their teaching practicums is presented.

4.1 About the school

This study was conducted in the 2nd grade class at an elementary school attached to an education university. All students from the university conduct their teaching practicums at this elementary school. In this school, English is taught not only to 5th and 6th grade students, but also to 1st, 2nd, 3rd, and 4th grade students once per week. Each grade has three classes, and there are 32 students per class. I was an HRT for the 2nd grade class and an instructor for the teaching practicum in 2013. This school had an ALT, so teachers were able to teach English in team-teaching (TT) with the ALT.

4.2 Participants

The participants were five pre-service teachers (PST-A, PST-B, PST-C,

PST-D, and PST-E) who were 3rd year students at the university. I explained the study purpose and obtained the informed consent of the participants. Table 4.1 provides the background of the pre-service teachers.

Table 4.1
Background of the Pre-Service Teachers

Pre-service teachers	Gender	Major field	Experience of learning English before junior high school
PST-A	M	Japanese	None
PST-B	M	Mathematics	None
PST-C	F	Arts and Crafts	None
PST-D	F	Music	None
PST-E	F	Science	None

4.3 The teaching practicum schedule

The teaching practicum of the pre-service teachers was carried out over four weeks, from October 15 to November 8, 2013. The pre-service teachers observed and conducted not only English lessons but also other subject lessons because elementary school teachers teach all subjects in Japan. However, in this paper, I focused on teaching English.

In the 1st week (October 15-October 18), the pre-service teachers observed two English lessons given by the HRT. One of them was conducted in TT with the ALT. Observing these lessons was important in the teaching practicum because the pre-service teachers had not previously observed English lessons at elementary schools. PST-A wrote "I do not have any images of English lessons at elementary schools" in the questionnaire conducted at the beginning of the teaching practicum. This was due to the fact that teaching English at elementary schools was not part of the elementary school curriculum when the participating pre-service teachers attended. In addition, none of them had taken a course on teaching English at elementary schools yet at the university. This situation is the same as that observed in the reports of Uchino (2015) and Kasuya et al. (2014) in the literature review. The HRT's lesson topic was "Do you like vegetables?" The pre-service teachers had discussions, including with the HRT, after school on those two days.

During the 2nd week (October 21-October 25), the pre-service teachers planned and taught their individual lessons. Each pre-service teacher taught one English lesson. They discussed the lessons with the HRT before and after each pre-service teacher conducted a lesson. The pre-service teachers' lesson titles are shown in the list below. These topics are from the school's curriculum, and were not chosen by the pre-service teachers. They adapted their lesson plans according to the curriculum.

PST-A, PST-B, PST-C: "What subject do you like?"
PST-D, PST-E: "Let's act a play."

In the 3rd week (October 28-November 1), the pre-service teachers began collaborative lesson study. They set goals and planned the procedures of the unit and each lesson. They jointly developed the lesson unit shown below. Each pre-service teacher was assigned one lesson of the unit. The pre-service teachers had discussions five times, including with the HRT, during this week. At the beginning of the week, the pre-service teachers developed a unit titled "What time is it?" The main activity involved students asking each other "What time is it?" using the time mentioned on the distributed cards. During the discussion, the HRT facilitated collaborative thinking by asking, "What do you know about the objective of Foreign Language Activities written in the Course of Study?" and "What do you mean by communication?" They also offered their insights during the discussions. The pre-service teachers realized that communication allowed them to exchange new information, and the discussion led them to change the topic of the unit to "What time do you get up?" They realized that just having children say phrases in English to each other was repetitive practice, not authentic communication, because no new message was exchanged. The HRT adjusted the pre-service teachers' discussion and played the role of MKO. This role is important in a teaching practicum because pre-service teachers do not have much teaching experience yet.

Lesson Plan

Title   Let's ask times of our daily routine

Goals
  *Enjoy coming to know friends' times of their daily routine.
  *Ask about and answer questions regarding daily routine and time in English.
  *Know difference between English and loan words.

Procedure of the unit
  1 Learn English words regarding daily routine (PST-D)
  2 Learn English words regarding time (PST-E)
  3 Ask each other "What time do you get up?" (PST-C)
  4 Ask each other "What time do you go to school?" (PST-B)
  5 Ask each other "What time do you go to bed?" (PST-A) [**Research lesson**]

Procedure of the research lesson (PST-A)
  1 Greetings
  2 Pronunciation of daily routine terms
  3 Game "Simon says"
  4 Song "What time do you get up?"
  5 Ask each other "What time do you go to bed?"
  6 Share information from No.5
  7 Reflection

In the 4th week (November 5-November 8), each pre-service teacher conducted an assigned lesson from the unit that they developed together. The process was carried out in a manner such that when one conducted a lesson, the others observed it, and then they all discussed it to refine the next lesson plan. They discussed the lessons before and after each pre-service teacher conducted a lesson. As the final step, one of them (PST-A) opened a lesson (referred to as a research lesson) to the other classes' pre-service teachers and HRTs, and afterward there was a post-lesson discussion.

4.4 Data collection and analysis

Data collection and analysis were carried out using M-GTA (Kinoshita, 2003, 2007) (see Chapter 3, section 3.1). For *theoretical sampling*, an open-ended questionnaire ("What do you think about teaching English at elementary schools?") and follow-up interviews (15 minutes, one on one) were collected as data. During the teaching practicum, the pre-service teachers' logs, my field notes, and video recordings of the pre-service teachers' discussions were collected. The number of recorded discussions was 17, and each was about 30 minutes long (total: eight and a half hours). The pre-service teachers wrote a log every day. At the end of the teaching practicum, an open-ended questionnaire ("What do you think about teaching English at elementary schools?") and follow-up interviews (15 minutes, one on one) were collected. In addition, video recordings of the pre-service teachers' lessons, their practice lessons, and the post-lesson discussion were collected. The pre-service teachers' lesson plans were also collected for triangulated data to show qualitative rigor. All data were collected in Japanese and the results were translated into English.

In M-GTA, the data were transcribed, and then patterns showing similarity were gathered and given concept names. Concepts were labeled using < > symbols. In the *constant comparative* method, data are gathered, analyzed, and compared against previously collected data. First, I developed three concepts from the open-ended questionnaire and follow-up interviews from the beginning of the teaching practicum. Those concepts are <Alphabet>, <Only songs and games>, and <Anxiety>. I continually checked videos of the pre-service teachers' discussions, their logs, and my field notes every day during their practicums to compare them against previous data to add examples to the analysis worksheets or to develop new concepts. During this procedure, I discovered new concepts: <Guessing>, <English knowledge>, <A lot of English>, <Instructional skills>, and <Understanding children's situations>. I analyzed the open-ended questionnaire and follow-up interviews at the end of the teaching practicum as well. I added more examples to the analysis worksheets and developed another new concept, <Collaboration>. Finally, I examined the video recordings of the pre-service teachers' lessons, their practice lessons, and the post-lesson discussion. I also checked their lesson plans and confirmed no more data could be derived. I developed nine concepts during this stage.

As stated in Chapter 3, I asked my co-worker to develop concepts from the transcripts as well, as peer-debriefing. She came up with eight concepts: <Listening>, <Guessing>, <A lot of English>, <Understanding children's situations>, <Understanding communication>, <Deepen one's thoughts>, <Positive feeling>, and <Help each other>. We both came up with <Guessing>, <A lot of English>, and <Understanding children's situations>. Some concepts she developed were different from mine, so we discussed which were better. I then added <Listening>, <Positive feeling>, and <Understanding communication> and adopted <Deepen one's thoughts> and <Help each other> in place of <Collaboration> based on her feedback. I kept <Alphabet>, <Only

Chapter 4 Study on pre-service teachers   59

songs and games>, <Anxiety>, <English knowledge>, and <Instructional skills>. In addition, we checked frequent words and co-occurrence networks using KH Coder Ver.2 (see Appendices 2 & 3). We then added <Grammar>, <Course of Study>, <Flexibility>, and <Time control> in place of <Instructional skills> (open coding, see Chapter 3, section 3.5). In the next step, I made categories and labeled them using [ ] symbols (selective coding). I investigated the relationship between the categories. Several concepts were integrated into each category. I

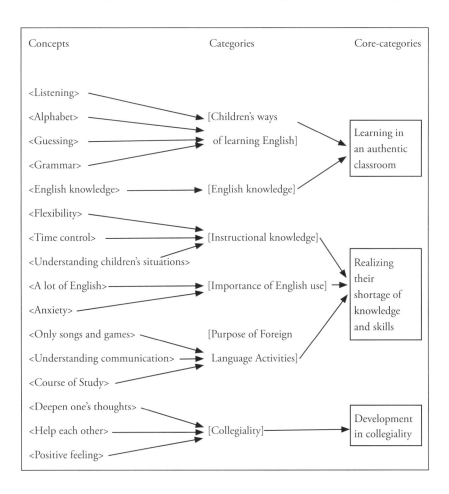

showed the concepts and categories to my co-worker, and she advised me to make core-categories, which are shown in boxes in the diagram below. Then we confirmed that we could come up with no more new concepts or categories, which helped us determine that *theoretical saturation* had been reached.

Finally, I made a diagram and a storyline and showed them to my co-worker. She gave me feedback regarding writing a procedure for the practicum beside the concepts and categories to show their developmental process (see Figure 4.1).

4.5 Results and discussion

Three core-categories and six categories emerged through comparative analysis of the data gathered from the participants. The core-categories are "Learning in an authentic classroom," "Realizing their shortage of knowledge and skills," and "Development in collegiality." Under "Learning in an authentic classroom," there are two categories, which are (1) [Children's ways of learning English] and (2) [English knowledge]. Under "Realizing their shortage of knowledge and skills," there are three categories, which are (3) [Instructional knowledge], (4) [Importance of English use], and (5) [Purpose of Foreign Language Activities]. In "Development in collegiality," there is one category, (6) [Collegiality]. Figure 4.1 indicates how the core-categories, categories, and concepts are related. This shows the developmental process of the pre-service teachers.

Chapter 4 Study on pre-service teachers   61

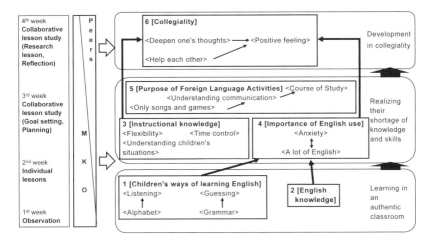

Figure 4.1. The developmental process of pre-service teachers

---

Storyline

In the first week, the pre-service teachers observed the HRT's lessons. They were able to observe [Children's ways of learning English], especially children's <Listening> and <Guessing> abilities. They changed their beliefs regarding <Alphabet> and <Grammar>. They also gained [English knowledge] of familiar English words and practical expressions. "Learning in an authentic classroom" had an impact on the pre-service teachers.

In the second week, the pre-service teachers conducted individual lessons and were able to learn [Instructional knowledge]. They struggled in conducting their lessons and recognized their lack of <Flexibility> and <Time control>, as well as the necessity of <Understanding children's situations>. They also learned the [Importance of English use]. Although they understood that they should use <A lot of English> in a lesson, they felt <Anxiety> when using English with the children.

In the third week, they started their collaborative lesson study, which involved making one lesson unit together. During their discussions, they realized [Purpose of Foreign Language Activities], supported by the HRT. First, they thought that activities were <Only songs and games>. However, after <Understanding communication>, they understood the purpose of Foreign Language Activities in the <Course of Study>. In the second and third weeks, "Realizing their shortage of knowledge and skills" occurred.

In the fourth week, they conducted a research lesson and had a post-lesson discussion in their collaborative lesson study. At this stage, they came to recognize [Collegiality]. They were able to <Deepen one's thoughts> and <Help each other> in their peer interactions. In the end, they had a <Positive feeling> about teaching English. They had "Development in collegiality."

4.5.1 Category (1) [Children's ways of learning English]

Category (1) [Children's ways of learning English] is supported by four concepts: <Listening>, <Alphabet>, <Guessing>, and <Grammar>. When the pre-service teachers realized that children were good at <Listening> and <Guessing>, they realized that children learned English in different ways from the traditional approaches to learning. At that point, their beliefs that <Alphabets> and <Grammar> should be taught changed.

4.5.1.1 Concept of <Listening>

When the pre-service teachers observed the HRTs' lessons, they were surprised that children listened to and understood English well. The comments below correspond with this concept.

> I was surprised that children raised their hands just after the teacher's "Anyone?" I could not catch the teacher's English words. (PST-A, October 17, discussion)

> The children could sing an English song they listened to for the first time. Did you understand the words of the song that the children sang? I did not understand. (PST-B, October 17, discussion)

> The children's listening ability is great. I could not catch what the teacher said. She said "If …, discuss …" What did she say? The children's listening ability is unbelievable. (PST-C, October 18, discussion)

The pre-service teachers did not learn English in their elementary school days. This was the first time they had observed English lessons. They were surprised that the children understood the HRT's English speech, which they (university students) did not understand, and thought that the children's listening abilities were better than their own. This changed their beliefs, which is shown in the next concept.

4.5.1.2 Concept of <Alphabet>

The pre-service teachers were surprised that the children learned English orally without knowing the alphabet. The comments below correspond with this concept.

> I wonder why the children can understand well without [knowing the] alphabet. They pronounced with native-like pronunciation. It is because of young age, isn't it? On the other hand, reading written English makes us pronounce with a Japanese accent. (PST-D, October 18, discussion)

> We need to look at written English to understand words, but children do not. Although I thought that the alphabet should be taught at the beginning, these children did not learn it. (PST-A, October 18, discussion)

In the questionnaire conducted at the beginning of the teaching practicum, PST-D wrote, "It's difficult to teach English without knowing the alphabet. It's insignificant to teach children English because they do not understand." This belief developed early on for the pre-service teacher because she started learning English in junior high school, and learning the alphabet was taught first when she was a student. Lortie (1975) contended that many beliefs teachers hold about teaching originate from their personal experiences as students (apprenticeship of observation). He asserted that prior learning experience in schooling played a crucial role in determining teaching beliefs and practices. Beliefs may outweigh the effects of teacher education (Kagan, 1992; Richardson, 1996) (see Chapter 2, section 2.2.2). However, when PST-D saw that the children could understand English without knowing the alphabet, her beliefs that children do not understand English and that letters of the alphabet should be taught first changed. Observing children's ways of learning English in an authentic classroom setting led to a shift in the teachers' way of thinking. This supports the result that teachers were affected by children's growth patterns (Nakayama, 2011, 2012).

4.5.1.3 Concept of <Guessing>

According to Brewster and Ellis (2002), children have a natural ability to grasp meaning from a variety of sources: body language, intonation, gesture, facial expression, and social context, as well as language itself. Children may not understand every word, but they can understand the meaning from the context, visuals, and gestures (Cameron, 2001). Children are skilled at guessing and predicting. The comments below correspond with this concept. PST-A, PST-B, PST-E, and PST-D realized that the children could guess what the teachers were saying.

I was impressed that the children guessed the meanings of English words without the teacher's translations or explanations. (PST-A, October 17, log)

The children could somehow understand English that they had not yet learned by understanding the situations. (PST-B, October 17, log)

Even if a teacher used slightly difficult English, the children could understand the meaning from the teacher's expressions and gestures. (PST-E, October 17, log)

Previously, I thought that children could not understand English without explanations or translations. Now, I know I was wrong about this. (PST-D, October 18, discussion)

The pre-service teachers thought that teachers should create chances for children to guess the meanings in lessons, as shown below:

The children were able to guess the meanings of English words from the teacher's gestures. It is important to make children guess the meanings of English words. (PST-B, October 18, discussion)

It is significant to develop the ability of guessing meanings. (PST-C, October 18, log)

Teachers should speak English almost all the time because children can understand English through teachers' gestures and expressions. (PST-D, October 18, log)

I understood that it was important to make children think about the meanings of English words through teachers' use of lots of English with gestures and expressions. (PST-E, October 18, discussion)

The awareness of learners' abilities contributed to the developmental process of the pre-service teachers when they compared the children's ways of learning English to their ways of learning. In the next concept, the process of realizing the difference is documented.

4.5.1.4 Concept of <Grammar>

PST-C and PST-E realized that children learn English in different ways from them, as seen below:

> We learned the grammar of "Do you like …?" in junior high school, but children do not. They can understand the meaning without an explanation of grammar or a translation. (PST-C, October 18, discussion)

> Children and the HRT use past tense, for example, "I forgot." We learned past tense after present tense in junior high school. (PST-E, October 18, discussion)

The pre-service teachers learned from a traditional method of teaching English through direct deductive explanations of grammar and remembering words one by one in junior and senior high school, as seen below:

> Teachers at my junior high school read English in a Japanese accent. English was not taught orally. Translations and grammatical points were taught mainly for tests. (PST-A, October 15, interview)

> When I was a student in junior high school and senior high school,

teachers explained grammar and translated from English to Japanese. (PST-B, October 15, interview)

I rarely had chances to pronounce English in my junior and senior high school days. The main focus was on learning grammar for tests. (PST-C, October 15, interview)

I always translated English in a textbook to Japanese, and then teachers gave a model of translations and explained grammatical points. It made me dislike English. (PST-D, October 15, interview)

I remembered the Japanese meanings of English words for tests, not for practical use, in my junior high school days. (PST-E, October 15, interview)

As is evidenced by these comments, they seem to be impressed that the children understood English inductively, without explanations or translations. After observing children's ways of learning English, the pre-service teachers recognized that lessons in elementary schools were focused on learning oral English. "Learning in an authentic classroom" had an impact on the pre-service teachers.

4.5.2 Category (2) [English knowledge]

Kawakami (2008) pointed out that most Japanese started learning English in their junior high school days, and many abstract words were taught. Because English was not part of the elementary school curriculum when the participating pre-service teachers attended, they may not have had much introduction to basic and familiar English words like giraffe, cucumber, stapler, etc. PST-A did not know how to say *horenso* [spinach] and *nasu* [eggplant] in English.

> I could not catch *horenso* [spinach]. How do you say *horenso* in English? I could not catch *nasu* [eggplant] either. (PST-A, October 17, discussion)

When PST-A asked, "How do you say *horenso* in English?" nobody answered. This is similar to the fact that they know countable nouns and uncountable nouns as knowledge, but they have never used them. PST-C did not know that we should say, "I like tomatoes," not "I like tomato." They also did not know that when we speak, for example, about broccoli, it is correct to say "I like broccoli," not "I like broccolis."

> I was reminded of countable nouns and uncountable nouns today. The HRT uses them correctly. (PST-B, October 18, discussion)

> The HRT corrected children's "I like tomato" to "I like tomatoes." Should we say "I like tomatoes?" (PST-C, October 18, discussion)

The pre-service teachers learned more English, as seen below:

> I learned the expressions "Let me try," "I'm finished," and "I forgot" when I watched the children using them in a lesson. (PST-A, October 17, discussion)

> We say "delicious," but I realized that children said "yummy." (PST-B, October 18, discussion)

The pre-service teachers learned these English words, expressions, and structures from observing the lesson. Teachers need to have some level of language proficiency. Knowledge of content is of critical importance (Koehler & Mishra, 2009). The pre-service teachers gained some English knowledge during this teaching practicum.

4.5.3 Category (3) [Instructional knowledge]

The pre-service teachers need not only content knowledge, in this case, English language proficiency, but also instructional knowledge of how to teach. Category (3) [Instructional knowledge] includes three concepts: <Flexibility>, <Time control>, and <Understanding children's situations>.

4.5.3.1 Concept of <Flexibility>

The pre-service teachers' limited classroom experiences may have made it difficult for them to anticipate student responses and misconceptions or to estimate appropriate timing of lesson elements (Burroughs & Luebeck, 2010). In the early stages of learning to teach, teachers tend to stick to a lesson plan (Sasajima, 2009). Senior (2006) also mentioned this issue:

> Pre-service teachers tend to view lessons as collections of discrete parts, rather than as integrated wholes. As yet unable to see which parts of the lesson are more vital than others, they are unsure whether or not to terminate an activity and move on to the next segment. (p. 43)

The pre-service teachers discovered that they had to deal with children's unexpected reactions with more flexibility. They realized that it was important to adapt themselves to the children's reactions. Below are comments about flexibility:

We have to think about how to deal with children's unexpected reactions. (PST-B, October 22, log)

We need to judge situations immediately because lessons are not carried out as planned. (PST-A, October 23, log)

I was flustered when I encountered unexpected things. I have to listen to the children's remarks. (PST-C, October 24, log)

I would like to react to the children's remarks with more flexibility. Although I always want to do what I planned, it is natural that children say unpredictable things. I do not have to persist with a lesson plan. (PST-E, October 24, discussion)

I could not deal with things that I could not predict. (PST-E, October 25, log)

We should always observe and understand children in order to pick up children's remarks well during a lesson. (PST-A, October 28, log)

I always looked at a lesson plan during a lesson. I would like to observe the children's reaction carefully. We did some micro-teaching at university before this teaching practicum. But real children are far different from those in our imagination. (PST-D, October 25, discussion)

As PST-D stated, pre-service teachers usually conduct some micro-teaching at university before their teaching practicums. However, conducting real lessons with real children had a strong impact on them. The pre-service teachers also thought their instructional skills were not strong enough. Evidence can be seen in the following comments from the participants:

> My voice was small and flat. I need to modulate it. (PST-C, October 22, discussion)

> We need to plan how to use the board. It is important to have children put only things they need on the desk. (PST-E, October 23, discussion)

> The children did not understand my instructions sometimes. I have to think about good instructions. (PST-B, October 24, discussion)

4.5.3.2 Concept of <Time control>

Sometimes pre-service teachers let the warm-up activities run on too long, forgetting that their function is simply a lead-in to the main part of the lesson (Senior, 2006). The pre-service teachers learned about time control. None of them could control time.

> I was in a hurry, so I could not properly observe the children's reactions. (PST-C, October 22, discussion)

> I was too hasty at the end of the lesson. (PST-E, October 22, discussion)

> I was surprised when I looked at the clock. A lot of content was still left

then. (PST-D, October 23, discussion)

We need to control time, we often run short. (PST-B, October 25, discussion)

I had needless pauses in my lesson. I should have given instructions in a crisp manner. (PST-C, October 25, log)

PST-A learned that teachers should allow more thinking time for children.

Children need time to think. If a teacher calls children's names quickly, they are deprived of their thinking time. Warm-up activities run on too long. (PST-A, October 24, discussion)

Keeping time and adapting to children's reactions (flexibility) are the main problems for pre-service teachers.

4.5.3.3 Concept of <Understanding children's situations>

The needs of children and how they learn must be the primary consideration (Brewster & Ellis, 2002). The pre-service teachers learned that it was important to be aware of children's learning situations and to set up teaching goals, topics, and activities with them in mind. Below are comments about this concept:

The HRT used things familiar to the children in their daily lives for topics, such as, vegetables the children grew. (PST-B, October 29, log)

The HRT's lesson plan is great. Teaching goals and activities are set up with children's learning situations in mind. I had thought that writing about children in a lesson plan was just a formality, and that I could copy a lesson plan from anywhere. But now I understand that we should be aware of children's situations while planning lessons. (PST-B, October 29, discussion)

PST-B recognized that a lesson plan was written with children's particular situations in mind, and that it is not advisable to just copy a lesson from anywhere. He also realized that the HRT selected vegetables as a meaningful topic because the children grew some vegetables, such as tomatoes, green peppers, and eggplant, in a life skills class. PST-A realized that understanding children's situations is significant in developing a lesson.

I made a lesson plan from only a teacher's view. It is important to make a lesson plan with an understanding of the children's situation. (PST-A, November 1, log)

PST-D and PST-E realized that decision-making and collaborative learning were effective for children.

The HRT let the children choose the words they wanted to say, which is one reason the children like English. (PST-D, October 18, discussion)

The HRT gave a lot of group activities for the children to help each other, so children who are weak at English could answer. (PST-D, October 18, discussion)

The HRT gave activities focused on learning things about each other. (PST-E, October 18, discussion)

[Instructional knowledge] is needed to teach all subjects. Developing this awareness through experiences is helpful in becoming a teacher. Different from in-service teachers, pre-service teachers learn [Instructional knowledge] and [English knowledge] simultaneously.

4.5.4 Category (4) [Importance of English use]

Category (4) [Importance of English use] includes two concepts, <A lot of English> and <Anxiety>. The pre-service teachers learned that teachers should use English as much as the circumstances allow. However, they felt anxious about their English competence.

4.5.4.1 Concept of <A lot of English>

Curtain and Dahlberg (2010) wrote that teachers should consistently conduct instruction in the target language with minimal use of the native language and translation. The pre-service teachers learned that it was important to use a lot of English in context from observing the HRT's lessons, as exemplified below:

The HRT says the key sentence "Do you like …?" many times in various activities so children can listen to the sentence many times unconsciously. (PST-A, October 17, discussion)

I was surprised that the HRT almost only used English. Teachers used a lot of Japanese to explain grammar in my junior high school days. (PST-C, October 18, discussion)

The HRT spoke English in context. That is why the children understand English well. (PST-D, October 18, discussion)

Lessons are conducted in English. The HRT mentioned that this was to enhance the opportunities for children to be exposed to English. When the children spoke in Japanese, the HRT reacted and answered in English. It makes lessons focus on real communication. (PST-E, October 18, discussion)

They realized that the HRT tried to skillfully use English as much as possible, so that the children would to be exposed to more English. However, they felt anxious about their English competence, as discussed in the next concept.

4.5.4.2 Concept of <Anxiety>

The pre-service teachers stated that they felt anxiety regarding teaching English in their interviews at the beginning of their teaching practicums. They mentioned that they worried about their lack of English competence, especially pronunciation. Teacher anxiety over teaching English was also reported by Nahatame (2014), Monoi (2013), and N. Matsumiya (2013) in the literature review (see Chapter 2, section 2.2). A perceived low level of language proficiency may be a considerable factor leading to teaching anxiety (Aydin, 2016). They did not want to teach in TT with an ALT. PST-C stated, "I would like to teach English by myself without an ALT because I cannot talk to an ALT in English." The pre-service teachers' comments on the difficulties of using English can be seen below:

> The HRT used English almost all the time with gestures, clear voice, emphasizing key expressions. It is hard to do that for me. (PST-A, October 17, discussion)

> I learned that teachers should speak English clearly using short sentences. I heard from the HRT that children tend to be noisy in English lessons compared to math or Japanese lessons. It is hard to be understood by the children while instructing in English. (PST-E, October 17, log)

> Although I practiced English a lot, I used a lot of Japanese in my lesson. (PST-E, October 23, discussion)

> I prepared English to use for the lesson, but I could not use English when children reacted in unexpected ways. (PST-B, October 24, discussion)

> We pre-service teachers use Japanese a lot. We do not have enough English competence yet. (PST-C, October 25, log)

> When I think to myself that I should be using English in a lesson, I cannot look at the children and my voice becomes small. (PST-B, October 25, discussion)

> I thought classroom English was easy before, but now I know it is difficult to use it in response to children's reactions. (PST-A, October 29,

log)

The pre-service teachers realized that it was difficult to use classroom English in response to children's reactions, even if they prepared and practiced. After observing the model lessons taught by the HRT and conducting their own lessons, the pre-service teachers realized that they did not have enough English competence yet. Itoi (2014), Tanaka et al. (2013), and Ikuma and Hosoda (2015) also reported that pre-service teachers realized their English proficiency was not high enough after their teaching practicums (see Chapter 2, section 2.2). This outcome shows that the pre-service teachers need to become familiar with English and find ways to reduce their anxiety about using classroom English.

4.5.5 Category (5) [Purpose of Foreign Language Activities]

English lessons at elementary schools in Japan were called Foreign Language Activities in 2013, when this teaching practicum was conducted. The category (5) [Purpose of Foreign Language Activities] is supported by three concepts: <Only songs and games>, <Understanding communication>, and <Course of Study>. Although the pre-service teachers previously thought <Only songs and games> were conducted in Foreign Language Activities, a breakthrough in their teacher thinking emerged as they began to understand what real communication is. They also began to understand the purpose of Foreign Language Activities in <Course of Study>.

4.5.5.1 Concept of <Understanding communication>

Real communication that has authentic information is important in language learning (Curtain & Dahlberg, 2010). Simply providing children with opportunities to learn and repeat new words will not develop communicative competence (Brewster & Ellis, 2002). The pre-service teachers realized what real communication is through interactions with and advice from the HRT. They then changed their unit topic regarding communication (see section 4.4). Below are comments about understanding communication:

Having the children ask each other "What time is it?" using cards is just practice, not communication. (PST-A, October 29, discussion)

Communication is to express our thoughts and feelings. (PST-E, October 30, log)

Communication is to be interested in one's remarks. Our first lesson plan was missing communication. (PST-B, October 31, log)

Communication is to know things about each other. I learned that exchanging information was important, not just practicing. (PST-C, October 31, log)

Communication is to know each other's feelings. Now I know real communication is important. Activities focused on learning things about each other through communication in English are good. (PST-D, November 1, discussion)

This supports the result that the pre-service teachers were affected by understanding the English lessons' communication principles (Nakayama, 2011, 2012). <Understanding communication> affected their understanding of <Course of Study>, as will be shown later.

4.5.5.2 Concept of <Only songs and games>

At the beginning of the teaching practicum, the pre-service teachers thought that Foreign Language Activities meant just fun games and songs or saying something orally. That is because only fun games and songs were used in "the Period for Integrated Studies." However, the picture has completely changed, as evidenced below:

> At first I thought it was OK to give some games and songs in Foreign Language Activities lessons, but now I know exchanging information is significant. (PST-B, October 28, log)

> I did not understand the meaning of communication. I thought saying something with a partner orally or playing some games was communication. But it did not include meaningful information. (PST-E, October 28, log)

> I thought it was OK to teach simple words and expressions through games, but now I do not think so. Exchanging information is crucial in communication. (PST-A, October 29, discussion)

The HRT acted as a great role model to lead their thinking in a dialogic nature.

4.5.5.3 Concept of <Course of Study>

The pre-service teachers already knew that the objective of Foreign Language Activities written in the national curriculum <Course of Study> was to form the foundation of children's communication abilities. However, they did not know the real meaning of "communication."

I thought that the Course of Study was just a formality, and teachers did not care about it before, but now I think it is very important. (PST-A, October 30, discussion)

I realized that I did not understand the Course of Study. The purpose of Foreign Language Activities is to enjoy communication, not to force memorization of words and expressions. (PST-B, October 31, discussion)

The most impressive thing in this teaching practicum is that our lesson plan was rejected by the HRT because real communication was not included in our plan. We did not understand the meaning of communication, which was the primary purpose of Foreign Language Activities. (PST-A, November 8, discussion)

My thoughts about Foreign Language Activities have completely changed. Now I understand that the purpose of Foreign Language Activities is communication, not remembering many words. (PST-D, October 29, discussion)

I had thought that the most important thing was acquiring English knowledge. But through making a lesson plan collaboratively, I understood that the learning process was significant. In a lesson, teachers should encourage children to think, not force them to remember things. (PST-C, October 31, log)

PST-E, PST-B, and PST-A realized that reading the national curriculum Course of Study and understanding the purpose of Foreign Language Activities were important. They realized their shortage of knowledge and skills at this stage.

4.5.6 Category (6) [Collegiality]

According to the National Association for the Study of Education Methods (2011), the core principle of lesson study is teacher collaboration. Numerous authors (Al-Weher, 2004; Fosnot, 1996; Graham, Hudson-Ross, & McWhorter, 1997; Gunstone, Slattery, Baird, & Northfield, 1993; Jadallah, 1996; Magliaro, Murphy, Sawyers, Altieri, & Nienkark, 1996; Sherman & MacDonald, 2007) have suggested that collegiality, social interaction, and the use of discourse were key experiences for pre-service teachers and teacher educators. In this study, category (6) [Collegiality] is substantiated and supported by three concepts: <Deepen one's thoughts>, <Help each other>, and <Positive feeling>.

4.5.6.1 Concept of <Deepen one's thoughts>

Regarding <Deepen one's thoughts>, the pre-service teachers worked out and deepened their thoughts through peers' advice. According to Segawa and Fukumoto (2006), successful collaboration leads to exchanging knowledge, creating new ideas, and forming objective views, and as a result, critical thinking occurs. They also mentioned that without collaboration, teachers might become defensive and try to justify their lessons. In this study, the pre-service teachers made one lesson unit collaboratively. The pre-service teachers deepened their knowledge of teaching and were able to constructively reflect on what they were doing through their peers' advice. Evidence showing the value of collegial peer advice can be seen in the following comments from the participants:

I could deepen my thoughts through saying my thoughts and listening to other pre-service teachers' thoughts. (PST-E, November 6, log)

I learned many things from peers' lessons. (PST-A, November 8, log)

Discussing among the pre-service teachers is meaningful. It is not good to ask the HRT for the answers so easily. (PST-B, November 8, interview)

New ideas and insights were shared. How to use picture cards effectively was new to me. (PST-D, November 8, interview)

We worked out thoughts and ideas through writing a lesson plan together. (PST-E, November 8, interview)

We had reflection meetings every day, so I could improve my lesson. (PST-A, November 7, log)

I received advice of what I should improve. (PST-E, November 7, discussion)

Knowledge is co-constructed in the dialogic nature of the discourse. The comments above point out that developing lessons collaboratively provides opportunities to share knowledge stemming from classroom practice and rich experience.

4.5.6.2 Concept of <Help each other>

The pre-service teachers realized that sharing information was helpful. They supported each other with time-keeping, which was one of their main concerns. They also helped each other regarding understanding children's situations, which they learned the importance of in this practicum. Evidence can be seen in the following comments:

> I was thankful for their advice on time-keeping. (PST-A, November 7, discussion)

> I received advice from peers about the difficulty of playing a game. I also received opinions from peers about children's expected reactions to the game. (PST-D, November 6, log)

> We shared information about children, which is very helpful in preparing lessons. (PST-C, November 7, discussion)

> It is very significant we share knowledge about children jointly. Our perspectives on children broadened. (PST-A, November 7, log)

The pre-service teachers tried to improve their recognized shortage of skills that had become apparent to them in the previous weeks. This shows evidence of their development.

4.5.6.3 Concept of <Positive feeling>

Tschannen-Moran, Woolfolk-Hoy, and Hoy (1998) suggested that the increased collaboration with supportive peers can support pre-service teachers when they seem to lose their self-confidence due to a lack of experience and self-efficacy. In this study, the pre-service teachers reduced their anxiety about teaching. This can be seen in the supporting concept of <Positive feeling>, especially as it pertains to pronunciation practice, about which they felt <Anxiety> in the previous weeks.

> We practiced classroom English many times. The practice lesson was helpful. I could communicate well in English. (PST-A, November 8, interview)

> I have confidence in my pronunciation now. (PST-C, November 8, interview)

> It was good that we practiced classroom English together. I could use classroom English in my lesson. (PST-D, November 8, log)

PST-A, PST-C, and PST-D were worried about their pronunciation in the questionnaire conducted at the beginning of the teaching practicum. However, over the course of the practicum, they responded positively to the collaborative lesson study experience and reduced their anxiety about pronunciation. Peer discussion had an affective impact. Further comments are below:

> We are a team. I did not feel lonely. (PST-B, November 5, log)

> Peers encouraged me, saying, "You can do it." That made me relieved. (PST-C, November 5, log)

We thought about this unit together. This is our lesson, not someone else's affair. In the practice lesson, the other pre-service teachers gave me advice such as "Don't look down" and "You are talking too long" and so on. (PST-A, November 7, discussion)

I could look through a unit, not just one lesson. I thought an English lesson at elementary school was a one-shot lesson before this teaching practicum. (PST-B, November 5, discussion)

The comments above related to collegiality show strong evidence that to make lessons collaboratively and observe and discuss them were very useful practices for the pre-service teachers' practicums. This supports the result that teachers were affected by colleagues' cooperation (Nakayama, 2011, 2012). Collegiality was a key experience for pre-service teachers. The pre-service teachers developed further as teachers by experiencing collegiality. Further comments from the participants support the claim.

I could break a deadlock through advice from members. I would like to use classroom English a lot in the future. I would like to commune with colleagues after I become a teacher. (PST-D, November 8, log)

I realized that I had fixed my thinking using peers' advice. Now I do not think that I should not teach English. (PST-C, November 8, interview)

In the comments PST-D and PST-C can be seen to have changed their thoughts. They mentioned that they would like to keep on learning with colleagues in the future. Collaboration among teachers not only adds to knowledge gain (new ideas and insights) regarding teaching, but it also has a positive impact by providing emotional support.

4.6 Summary of chapter

The pre-service teachers gained a better understanding of (1) [Children's ways of learning English], (2) [English knowledge], (3) [Instructional knowledge], (4) [Importance of English use], (5) [Purpose of Foreign Language Activities], and (6) [Collegiality] during their teaching practicums by observing children, planning and conducting lessons, and discussing their experiences and ideas with peers. As a whole, their developmental process moved from "Learning in an authentic classroom" to "Realizing their shortage of knowledge and skills" to "Development in collegiality." In the end, they reduced their anxiety and developed positive feelings toward learning more about teaching. Further discussion of the outcomes of the pre-service teachers is presented in Chapter 7.

Chapter 5

Preliminary study on in-service teachers

In this chapter, a preliminary study on in-service teachers' school-based lesson study is presented. The purpose is to provide context for how school-based lesson study is usually carried out. I participated in this school-based lesson study as one of the collaborators. Since there is a lack of studies on school-based lesson study, I saw it as an opportunity to provide data by documenting how teachers in a Japanese public elementary school work collaboratively through school-based lesson study. Data from the participants and my observations are presented.

5.1 About the school

The school for the preliminary study is a public elementary school. In 2012, there were about 770 students. Grades 1, 2, 3, and 5 had four classes each, and grades 4 and 6 had three classes each. There were also two classes for special needs. There were 31 full-time teachers at the time of this study. Table 5.1 shows the years of teaching experience of the full-time teachers.

Table 5.1

The Years of Teaching Experience among the Full-Time Teachers at the School (2012–2013 academic year)

Teaching experience	Number of full-time teachers
1 year–fewer than 5 years	9 (29.0 %)
5 years–fewer than 10 years	1 (3.2 %)
10 years–fewer than 15 years	3 (9.7 %)
15 years–fewer than 20 years	4 (12.9 %)
20 years–fewer than 25 years	2 (6.4 %)
25 years–fewer than 30 years	5 (16.1 %)
More than 30 years	7 (22.6 %)
Total	31

Although the percentage of teachers who had more than 25 years of experience was high, the percentage of teachers who had fewer than 5 years of experience was also substantial. The school board send an ALT to this school twice a week, so teachers were sometimes able to teach English with the ALT.

Since this school has been a sister school with a public elementary school in Korea since 1989, its curriculum includes studies on international understanding. The sister school has more experience teaching English because English has been part of the national curriculum longer in Korea than Japan. Consequently, the Japanese school in this study had been researching teaching English through school-based lesson study before it became part of the national curriculum. Whereas schools generally teach English to 5th and 6th graders, this school teaches English to students of all grades. This school, through school-based lesson study, not only focuses on teaching English but, like most schools, also places attention on teaching Japanese. Teachers are divided into two teams based on their requests. Table 5.2 shows the number of teachers in each team.

Table 5.2
Number of Teachers in English Team and Japanese Team per Grade Level

Grade	1	2	3	4	5	6
English	2	2	2	1	2	2
Japanese	2	2	2	2	2	1

The numbers of both teams are equal. The school has a research steering committee, which consists of representatives of both the English and the Japanese teams. The overall structure of the school research organization is shown in Figure 5.1.

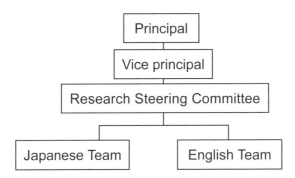

Figure 5.1. Structure of the school research organization (Preliminary Study). The research steering committee consists of representatives of the Japanese Team and the English Team and works with the principal and vice principal.

Both the English team and the Japanese team use lesson study and they open the lesson study to the other team twice per year, once for a head teacher's proposal lesson and once for an entire faculty research lesson. I was the head teacher of the English team. In this study, I focus only on the English team.

5.2 Procedures of the school-based lesson study

In this school, the after-school time period on Fridays is reserved for school-based lesson study. Teachers get together every Friday from 3:15 to 4:45. Below is the process of this school's school-based lesson study from April 2012 to March 2013.

Friday, April 20

The head teacher of the team proposed a theme to the entire faculty.

Friday, April 27

The team members discussed when they would do their own research lesson, and chose a teacher to be responsible for an entire faculty research lesson. Teacher A was selected because he had never yet done an entire faculty research lesson.

Thursday, May 10

The head teacher explained a plan for a proposal lesson to the entire faculty.

Friday, May 11

The head teacher's proposal lesson and a post-lesson discussion were held with the entire faculty.

Friday, May 18

The team members discussed the upcoming research lessons as a team.

Friday, June 8

Research lessons (3rd grade teacher and 1st grade teacher) and post-lesson discussions were held as a team.

Friday, July 6

The team members discussed the upcoming research lessons as a team.

Chapter 5 Preliminary study on in-service teachers **91**

Friday, July 13

Research lessons (4th grade teacher and 2nd grade teacher) and post-lesson discussions were held as a team.

Friday, September 7

The team members discussed the upcoming research lessons as a team.

Friday, September 14

Research lessons (5th grade teacher and 6th grade teacher) and post-lesson discussions were held as a team.

Friday, September 21

The team members discussed the upcoming research lessons as a team.

Friday, October 12

Research lessons (1st grade teacher and 5th grade teacher) and post-lesson discussions were held as a team.

Friday, November 16

The team members discussed the entire faculty research lesson as a team.

Friday, December 6

The team members discussed the entire faculty research lesson as a team again.

Thursday, December 13

Teacher A explained the plan for the entire faculty research lesson to the entire faculty.

Friday, December 14

The entire faculty research lesson (6th grade teacher, Teacher A) and a post-lesson discussion were held. In the post-lesson discussion, a supervisor from the school board provided feedback.

Friday, January 11

The team members discussed the upcoming research lesson as a team.

Friday, January 18

A research lesson (3rd grade teacher) and a post-lesson discussion were held as a team.

Friday, March 8

The team members reflected on this year's theme and lesson study in the entire faculty meeting.

Some research lessons were conducted in TT with the ALT. Every year, the school publishes one booklet, which included not only lesson plans but also some reflections of the teachers at the end of the year. Having a public open class that gives live research lessons is also common among Japanese public schools. However, this school did not conduct a public open class that year because they had conducted one the previous year.

5.3 Research lesson and post-lesson discussion

A post-lesson discussion is held on the same day as a research lesson for 75 minutes. Table 5.3 indicates the schedule followed by the school on those Friday afternoons.

Table 5.3
Schedule for a Research Lesson and a Post-Lesson Discussion

2:00-2:45	Research lesson
2:45-3:30	Students' dismissal
3:30-4:45	Post-lesson discussion

A post-lesson discussion starts with self-evaluation of the teacher who gives a research lesson. After other teachers ask questions about the lesson, teachers report the reactions of three selected children, and then they have a discussion. When it is an entire faculty research lesson, a supervisor invited from the school board provides feedback and final comments at the end of the discussion. At the prefecture and regional levels, there are individuals hired as supervisors. The role of a supervisor is to support the schools. They deliver support to a school by taking on the role of a lesson study advisor if the school happens to be conducting lesson study (Fernandez, 2002).

5.4 Findings

From this school's case, three factors stand out as being important for collaborative lesson study. They are "Leadership and shared roles," "All teachers give their own research lesson every year," and "Informal voluntary meetings."

5.4.1 Leadership and shared roles

The teachers at the school shared many responsibilities to make the lesson study go smoothly. First, the head teacher's role is important. At the beginning of the year, she proposed the following theme and focus to the faculty.

Research theme
To raise children who enjoy communication with people in English
Focus of study
To establish activities that promote meaningful interaction

She also proposed the ideas of students' goals for every grade, how to pick up topics, teaching procedures, and how to evaluate. Moreover, she gave a proposal lesson and a post-lesson discussion. From these two activities, members can consider prospective options for their own research lessons. During the year, the head teacher reported every lesson study to the faculty in the form of a newsletter. These newsletters allowed the teachers to share what was discussed. If they had questions and worries, they could ask the head teacher at anytime.

Second, other members shared many roles. In each stage of lesson plan development, the members of the team reviewed the lesson plan and provided feedback. The final version of the lesson plan was distributed to the faculty. During research lessons, they each took one specific role: taking pictures, taking a video, taking notes on the teacher's actions, and taking notes on three selected students' reactions. Before a research lesson, the teacher who conducted the research lesson selected students from whom the teacher expected strong, normal, and low performance. The teacher also prepared a sheet on which observation points were written and observers took notes. During a post-lesson discussion, they also shared and rotated the roles of facilitator and note-taker to record the discussion for the school's official record. These leadership and shared roles make lesson study collaborative.

5.4.2 All teachers give their own research lesson every year

As mentioned above, both the English team and the Japanese team do lesson study within their team, and they open lesson study to the other team twice a year, for the head teacher's proposal lesson and the entire faculty research lesson.

All HRTs do their own research lesson once a year, so each full-time teacher has the opportunity to be part of at least 13 research lessons, 11 lessons in their team and two lessons with the entire faculty, during the school year. Lesson study can be powerful even for teachers who just observe a research lesson and participate in the post-lesson discussion. This school system benefits teachers' development.

5.4.3 Informal voluntary meetings

Teacher A had two years of teaching experience and taught 6th graders that year. He conducted the entire faculty research lesson in December. To prepare the research lesson, first he decided on a topic and wrote a lesson plan. Then he proposed his plan to members in the English team meeting twice. Finally, he rewrote the lesson plan.

An additional aspect of teacher development at the school-one indirectly related to lesson study and demonstrating collaboration-is the unofficial or informal sharing of ideas. Teacher A asked his grade-level group teachers to share their opinions, even though one teacher was a member of the English team and the other teacher was a member of the Japanese team. Grade-level groups, meaning teachers who teach the same grades, are important in Japanese elementary schools to run school events and for academic activities. They have desks side by side in the teachers' room, and they have informal daily conversations of children's conditions and their worries about everyday instructions. The Japanese team teacher opened her class to Teacher A for a practice lesson. This allowed him to observe the children's reaction and the time-keeping needs and to adjust some parts. A head teacher visited to observe the practice lesson and gave some advice, also informally. It is not only Teacher A but all teachers who have these relationships with the same grade-level teachers. There are many of these kinds of informal voluntary meetings among teachers to help each other in Japanese schools.

5.5 Summary of chapter

The purpose of this chapter is to provide context for how school-based lesson study is typically carried out. Lesson study is part of the educational culture in Japan. In some countries, like the U.S., if teachers want to do lesson study, they must recruit group members and start lesson study on their own (see Chapter 2). In contrast, this preliminary study illustrates that school-based lesson study in Japan is highly structured and collaborative. From this school's case, three factors stand out as being important for collaborative lesson study. These are "Leadership and shared roles," "All teachers give their own research lesson every year," and "Informal voluntary meetings." The first factor was shown by the fact that, under the leadership of the head teacher, all teachers had various roles. The second factor pertains to the idea that all teachers give their own research lesson every year, as was seen in this lessons study, so they can be heavily involved throughout the course of the lesson study. The third factor relates to the idea of many informal, voluntary meetings. Although this is a case from one Japanese public elementary school, it shows how the teachers can work together for lesson study.

In the next chapter, the study on in-service teachers is presented. First, I describe their views on teaching English. Then, I present three lesson study cycles. Finally, I describe the developmental process of the teachers as they proceed through school-based lesson study.

Chapter 6
Study on in-service teachers

In this chapter, the study on in-service teachers is presented. First, the teachers' views on the inclusion of English in the national curriculum are presented. Then, I present three lesson study cycles. Finally, the developmental process of the in-service teachers is presented.

6.1 About the school

This study was conducted in a public elementary school in a different prefecture from the preliminary study. There is one class in each grade, for a total of six classes. This school became a "curriculum special school" for teaching English in April 2015. "Curriculum special schools" are designated by MEXT and have carried out plans to organize a curriculum that does not depend on the national curriculum. In April 2015, teachers in this school began teaching 35 English lessons per year (one lesson per week) as part of the school curriculum for 1st to 4th grade students, and 70 English lessons per year (two lessons per week) for 5th and 6th grade students. Teachers of the 1st and 2nd grades use the original curriculum that I designed. Teachers of the 3rd and 4th grades use, "Hi, friends!" distributed by MEXT. Teachers of the 5th and 6th grades use a course book, "LET'S GO," which is usually used in private schools. All English lessons are conducted through TT with an ALT. TT between a Japanese teacher and an ALT is one of the main teaching styles in English language education in elementary schools (Machida, 2016). Although the teachers in the preliminary study (see Chapter 5) focused not only on teaching English, but also on teaching Japanese, teachers in this school focus exclusively on teaching English. This school also has a research steering committee, which consists of representatives of a lower grade team and an upper grade team. Teachers from similar grades often come together to form one of these sub groups. The overall structure of the school research organization is shown in Figure 6.1.

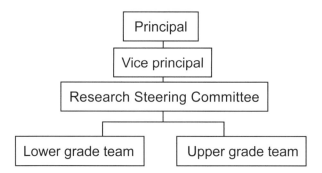

Figure 6.1. Structure of the school research organization. The research steering committee consists of the representatives of a lower grade team and an upper grade team, and works with a principal and a vice principal.

6.2 Participants

The participants were six HRTs in the elementary school (A, B, C, D, E, F). This is a small school and these six are all of the school's HRTs. I explained the study purpose and obtained the informed consent of the participants. The HRTs were not specialized in teaching English. Some of them had never taught English or received any training in teaching English. These participants suit this study because one of the purposes of this study is to gain a deeper understanding of in-service teachers who have not had experience or training in teaching English. Table 6.1 provides their background.

Table 6.1
Background of the In-service Teachers

Participant	Gender	Total years teaching	Years teaching English	Grade in charge	Experience taking training for English
A (Head teacher)	F	10 years	1 year	5th grade	Once
B	F	26 years	11 years	1st grade	None
C	F	4 years	4 years	3rd grade	None
D	F	4 years	None	2nd grade	None
E	M	27 years	4 years	6th grade	Once
F	M	30 years	4 years	4th grade	None

Although all of the teachers except Teacher D have experience teaching English, they mostly relied on ALTs for preparing and conducting lessons. They had not planned and taught English lessons by themselves.

6.3 Procedures of the school-based lesson study

This study was conducted from April 2015 to March 2016. Table 6.2 indicates the procedures of the school-based lesson study and of this study.

Table 6.2

Procedures of the School-Based Lesson Study and of this Study

Date	School-based lesson study	This study
April 15	I gave a lecture about the purpose of Foreign Language Activities and proposed a curriculum for this school.	Each teacher was asked to answer an open-ended questionnaire.
May 1	Teacher A (head teacher) proposed a theme to the entire faculty. The vice principal gave a lesson on classroom English.	
May 25	Teacher C gave a presentation about her experiences teaching English in another city.	
May 27		Interview 1 (Teachers A, B, and C)
June 5		Interview 1 (Teachers D and E)
June 17	I showed a video of teaching that MEXT distributed to all elementary schools and explained some teaching points.	
June 24		Interview 1 (Teacher F)
July 22	Teacher A reported on another elementary school's lesson that she had observed. Teacher D reported on a seminar that she had attended. The vice principal gave a lesson on classroom English. Teachers discussed the ALT, reading picture books, and instruction of alphabets. Teacher A proposed a format for a lesson plan.	
August 20	The vice principal conducted a workshop about phonics and classroom English.	
August 31	**Lesson study 1** (Planning) Teacher C proposed her lesson plan, and all the teachers discussed it.	
October 7	**Lesson study 1** (The research lesson of Teacher C and the post-lesson discussion)	I observed the research lesson and participated in the post-lesson discussion.

October 19	**Lesson study 2** (Planning) Teacher D proposed her lesson, and all the teachers discussed it.	I participated in the planning discussion.
October 26	**Lesson study 2** (The research lesson of Teacher D and the post-lesson discussion)	I observed the research lesson and participated in the post-lesson discussion.
January 20	**Lesson study 3** (Planning) Teacher E proposed his lesson, and all the teachers discussed it.	(I was invited to participate in the planning discussion, but I could not attend because of heavy snow.)
January 26	**Lesson study 3** (The research lesson of Teacher E and the post-lesson discussion)	I observed the research lesson and participated in the post-lesson discussion.
February 17	Teachers reflected on their school-based lesson study from the year.	
March 10		Interview 2 (Teachers B and D)
March 11		Interview 2 (Teachers C and F)
March 15		Interview 2 (Teachers A and E)
March 31	Teachers published a booklet regarding the results of the year.	

The teachers not only conducted three lesson study cycles, but also carried out their respective roles in the school-based lesson study. Teacher A (a head teacher) proposed a study theme and a lesson plan format, and all members discussed them. The teachers shared information, such as the professional development seminars they attended and the lesson study used at another school. The vice principal, who had been a junior high English teacher, shared his expertise. The teachers asked either the ALT or the vice principal to teach them classroom English and then took lessons. Finally, the teachers reflected on their one-year school-based lesson study and published a booklet, which included not only lesson plans but also their own reflections. I was a lecturer at a university that is in the same city of the elementary school, and I participated in their school-based lesson study as an MKO. I gave advice, answered requests, raised questions, and shared expertise.

6.4 In-service teachers' views on teaching English

In this section, I describe collected data and results regarding concepts, categories, and core-categories that emerged concerning teachers' views on teaching English.

6.4.1 Data collection and analysis

Data collection and analysis were carried out using M-GTA, developed by Kinoshita (2003, 2007) (see Chapter 3, section 3.1). During *theoretical sampling*, responses from questionnaires and interviews were collected as data. Each teacher was asked to answer an open-ended questionnaire on April 15, 2015. The questionnaire included the following three items:

1. What do you think about teaching English at elementary schools?
2. What do you think about your teaching English?
3. What is your conception of an ideal English lesson?

After receiving their questionnaire responses, one-on-one and semi-structured interviews were conducted in order to better understand the responses to the questionnaire or to seek more detailed explanations on the following schedule:

May 27, 2015   Teachers A, B, C

June 5, 2015   Teachers D, E

June 24, 2015   Teacher F

Each interview lasted approximately one hour. The interviews were electronically recorded with the consent of the participants. Data were transcribed in full in

Japanese and the results were translated into English.

Using M-GTA, I developed three concepts from the open-ended questionnaire: <Really needed?>, <Anxiety>, and <Ideal lesson>. I analyzed the interview data from Teachers A, B, and C and compared them against previous data to add examples to the analysis worksheets or to develop new concepts. I developed the following new concepts: <HRT's roles in TT>, <ALTs are needed>, and <Manuals are needed>. Then I analyzed the interview data from Teachers D, E, and F in the same manner. I added <Demonstration>, <Good learner model>, and <No image> in place of <HRT's roles in TT>. During the procedure, I came up with eight concepts total.

As stated in Chapter 3, I asked my co-worker to develop concepts from the transcripts as peer-debriefing. She came up with six concepts: <Repelling top-down manner>, <Ideal lesson>, <HRT's roles>, <ALTs>, <Manuals>, and <Internationalization>. The concepts we developed were almost the same, but some were different, so we discussed which were better. In addition, we checked frequent words and co-occurrence networks using KH Coder Ver.2 (see Appendices 5 & 6). I then added <Internationalization> and <Repelling top-down manner> and adopted <Concerning with other subjects> in place of <Really needed?>; I kept the other previous concepts. This gave us a total of ten concepts (Open coding, see Chapter 3, section 3.2). In the next step, I created categories and labeled them using [ ] symbols (Selective coding). Several concepts were integrated into each category. I showed the concepts and categories to my co-worker, and she advised me to create core-categories, which are given in the boxes as below. We then confirmed that we could come up with no more new concepts or categories, which helped us determine that *theoretical saturation* had been reached.

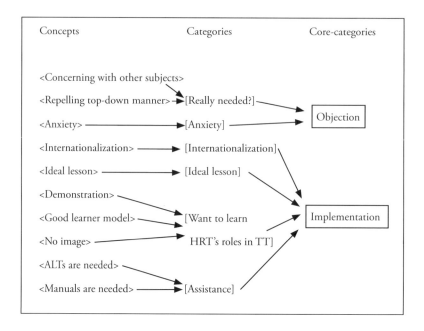

Finally, I made a diagram and a storyline and showed them to my co-worker. She gave me feedback, suggesting I draw an arrow to show conflict between "Objection" and "Implementation" in the diagram (see Figure 6.2).

6.4.2 Results and discussion

All concepts, categories, and core-categories were depicted in a diagram (Figure 6.2). The diagram indicates the two core-categories as "Objection" and "Implementation." Under "Objection," there are two categories: (1) [Really needed?] and (2) [Anxiety]. Under "Implementation," there are four categories: (3) [Internationalization], (4) [Ideal class], (5) [Want to learn HRT's role in TT], and (6) [Assistance].

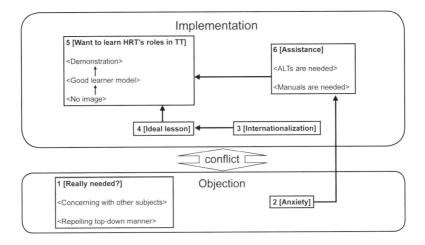

Figure 6.2. In-service teachers' views on teaching English

Storyline

The in-service teachers had a strong "Objection" to teaching English in elementary schools. They questioned, "Is it [Really needed?]" because they were <Concerning with other subjects> and <Repelling top-down manner>. They also felt [Anxiety] regarding their lack of English competence.

On the other hand, they understood the need for "Implementation" because of [Internationalization]. They had images of an [Ideal lesson] and they [Want to learn HRT's roles in TT]. Some teachers had <No image>, some teachers tried to be a <Good learner model>, and some teachers knew that they should do <Demonstration> of new expressions with an ALT. They thought <ALTs are needed> and <Manuals are needed> to start teaching English lessons because of their lack of confidence. There is conflict in their minds between "Objection" and "Implementation."

6.4.2.1 Category (1) [Really needed?]

Category (1) [Really needed?] consists of two concepts: <Concerning with other subjects> and <Repelling top-down manner>. The in-service teachers opposed English education at elementary schools. There were several reasons. The discussion begins with the concept of <Concerning with other subjects>.

6.4.2.1.1 Concept of <Concerning with other subjects>

The most common opposition is that students should learn Japanese reading and writing first rather than English (Nishida, 2006). Kusumoto (2008) also discussed this issue:

> Many teachers were concerned about students' proficiency and ability in Japanese language and the negative influence of second language learning on students' first language development such as "Japanese is more important than English" and "Students need to develop Japanese first." Many teachers believe English can be learned after the students fully develop their Japanese proficiency. (p. 30)

Teacher C stated that Japanese language education was more important than English language education.

> I oppose English education in elementary schools. Japanese education is more important than English education. Children do not have enough Japanese competence yet. If the number of English lessons increases, the number of Japanese lessons will decrease. (Teacher C, May 27, Interview 1)

Those who are opposed to English education in elementary schools have consistently said that we should teach students Japanese before English. Teacher F stated that there were new problems in education, such as special needs education and a decline in academic ability. He felt that those issues were more important than English teaching.

Declining academic ability has become a social problem nowadays. Lower-level children will have a heavy burden if the number of English lessons increases. Special needs education is more important than English education. (Teacher F, June 24, Interview 1)

Lower academic ability was widely discussed together with English education at elementary schools by the public (Nishida, 2006). Kusumoto (2008) mentioned that "some teachers also believe that there are more important issues to be taught such as moral education and the importance of life because of the increasing number of children committing suicide after being bullied" (pp. 30-31). Teacher C mentioned that elementary school teachers were busy teaching other subjects.

I do not want to take much time to prepare English lessons because teachers are busy teaching other subjects. (Teacher C, May 27, Interview 1)

This is a peculiar problem for elementary school teachers that does not exist for English teachers at the junior and senior high schools because in Japan, elementary school teachers teach all subjects.

6.4.2.1.2 Concept of <Repelling top-down manner>

A form of the verb "repel" was selected as the nomenclature for the concept because of the participants' strong resistance to the mandated policy. Nagamine's (2012) view spoke directly to teachers' reactions to the new policy:

The new language education policy was developed and introduced abruptly by MEXT in a top-down fashion, and that the new policy did not reflect EFL teachers' realities in local school settings. Voices of such critical stakeholders as pre-service and in-service EFL teachers (people who hold less power) are rarely heard. (p. 124)

Kusumoto (2008) mentioned the same issue as below, citing Butler (2007a):

Implementing new language policies in Japan has always resulted from top-down decisions without explicit directions from the government (Butler, 2007a). Consequently, it seems that the opinions of the teachers and the schools that are directly influenced by the new policy were not considered. (p. 2)

Teachers E and F complained that policy was developed in a top-down manner, as seen below.

Teachers have not had time to discuss why English education is needed in public elementary schools. The policy came in a top-down manner suddenly, without our discussion. (Teachers E, June 5, Interview 1)

I doubt whether English education in elementary schools is really needed. The government [MEXT] is pushing this policy by force. The government is nurturing people who can play an active role amid intensifying international competition. Is that really for all Japanese people? The government advances this policy without democratic procedure. Children from rich families will be able to attend cram schools for English. It is not for every child. (Teacher F, June 24, Interview 1)

The introduction of English education in elementary schools has been strongly requested in reaction to economics and globalization (Nishida, 2006). The in-service teachers opposed English education in elementary schools because they thought that Japanese and new problems in education were more important than English education, and they were busy teaching other subjects. For these reasons, there was resistance to the government's top-down policy.

6.4.2.2 Category (2) [Anxiety]

The next category is [Anxiety]. Researchers (e.g., Price, 1991; Williams & Andrade, 2008) argued that speaking English in front of others was the most anxiety-provoking activity for nonnative speakers. Anxious teachers tend to avoid using the target language in class (Horwitz, 1996). Butler (2007a) found that approximately 60% of Japanese elementary school teachers supported the idea that English should be taught by teachers with native-English-speaking proficiency. Teachers A, C, D, and E stated that they were not good at English pronunciation. Teacher F stated that he experienced difficulty dealing with foreigners.

I think I should be able to speak English fluently, but I cannot. That makes me feel anxious. I have watched some lessons in other schools over the past five years in which HRTs spoke well. I came to the keen realization that my English competence was insufficient. I have no confidence in my English pronunciation. (Teacher A, May 27, Interview 1)

I am not good at English and I have anxiety regarding pronunciation.

In particular, listening is hard, and I do not like to speak in English. Speaking English in public is hard for me. I always think that my pronunciation may be wrong, and that makes my voice small. (Teacher C, May 27, Interview 1)

I am not good at English, so I do not like English. I cannot say any English words. My pronunciation might not be acceptable. When I pronounced "sad," the ALT said "No." I feel a lot of anxiety. My pronunciation has a Japanese accent. Can I teach English to children? I do not know very much grammar. I cannot use verbs. I usually say only nouns. I have a poor vocabulary, so I cannot say any English. (Teacher D, June 5, Interview 1)

It is impossible to teach English for me. It is harmful to let children listen to my pronunciation. I cannot be a good model. (Teacher E, June 5, Interview 1)

I am not good at English. I also feel difficulty dealing with foreigners. (Teacher F, June 24, Interview 1)

In the comments above, a clear pattern emerged, as all of the teachers had high anxiety regarding their lack of English competence, especially their pronunciation. Their comments correspond with reports of HRTs' anxieties in the literature review (see Chapter 2, section 2.2). However, Machida (2016) mentioned the following:

Even nonnative language teachers with a good command of English or professional training were not confident about using the target language. It is plausible that Japanese elementary school teachers who are new to English language education are anxious about using English for classroom instruction. (p. 43)

MEXT requests that HRTs perform the role of a good model for learners. One of the main purposes of teacher development regarding teaching English is to reduce their anxiety.

6.4.2.3 Category (3) [Internationalization]

Nishida (2006) mentioned the following about globalization:

Many Japanese have been exposed to rapid globalization in recent years, and they have been forced to interact with foreign countries and non-native speakers of Japanese in various fields. We are expected to thoroughly master practical English in many areas of our daily lives. (p. 83)

The in-service teachers understood [Internationalization]. Teachers A, B, and C mentioned that they needed to use English in the age of internationalization, as seen below:

I understand that English is very much needed in our society. Many foreigners come to Japan. We need to communicate with them. English is also needed for jobs. (Teacher A, May 27, Interview 1)

English is needed due to recent globalization. (Teacher B, May 27,

Interview 1)

> English education is needed because it is a trend of the times. All Japanese say that we should learn practical English. We cannot resist the situation. (Teacher C, May 27, Interview 1)

> English education in elementary schools is meaningful in reforming the traditional style of English education, moving away from English for tests or just knowledge. (Teacher E, June 5, Interview 1)

Teacher E mentioned that improvement of English education in Japan was needed. He thought that practical English teaching was needed instead of the grammar-translation method in which he learned. The Japanese have a psychological complex about English conversation, and they want to speak English (Nishida, 2006). This outcome is related to the next concept, [Ideal lesson]. Although the teachers opposed English teaching in elementary schools, they also thought it was a necessity.

6.4.2.4 Category (4) [Ideal lesson]

The next category is [Ideal lesson]. The in-service teachers had the following thoughts on ideal lessons:

> I would like the children to communicate without hesitating. I want to be able to speak English and use a lot of English in lessons. I would like to communicate with the ALT well. (Teacher A, May 27, Interview 1)

> The goal is to be able to make daily conversation in English, not

grammar-translation. It is important that the children become familiar with English. It is also important that the children like learning English. It is not good to translate English to Japanese. I would like the children to understand in English and react in English. (Teacher B, May 27, Interview 1)

I would like the children to think that speaking English is interesting. I want to grow my English competence in order to teach. (Teacher D, June 5, Interview 1)

The ideal lesson is one through which children learn English with joy. I would like to teach useful expressions. I want the children to like English for communication, not for entrance examinations. I would like the children to learn English through communication. (Teacher E, June 5, Interview 1)

Teachers A, B, D, and E mentioned that they want children to learn English through communication with joy. Teacher B mentioned that daily English is important, not teaching grammar and translation. She rebelled against the idea of the traditional teaching style of English with which she was taught. Teachers A and D mentioned that they would like to learn English and speak it in lessons. Although they felt anxiety, they wanted to improve their English competence.

6.4.2.5 Category (5) [Want to learn HRT's roles in TT]

Category (5) [Want to learn HRT's roles in TT] consists of three concepts: <No image>, <Good learner model>, and <Demonstration>. The in-service teachers wanted to know their roles in TT for the first step. The discussion begins with the concept of <No image>.

6.4.2.5.1 Concept of <No image>

Teacher B stated that she did not have images of English lessons at elementary schools, so she wanted to observe an English lesson. This is because the teachers have had little chance to undergo teacher training.

> I do not have images of the HRT's roles in TT. I need something to have images. (Teacher B, May 27, Interview 1)

Teachers B and F mentioned that they did not know what roles they should perform in TT.

> I do not know the HRT's role in TT. When the ALT conducts lessons, how do I act? (Teacher B, May 27, Interview 1)

> I do not know the HRT's roles in TT. (Teacher F, June 24, Interview 1)

Teachers A and C mentioned that they did nothing in TT because the ALT taught English well enough.

> The ALT conducts lessons by himself. I do nothing. (Teacher A, May 27, Interview 1)

> The ALT can conduct everything. I do not do anything. He goes through lessons without me. I do not have any roles in English lessons. (Teacher C, May 27, Interview 1)

At this stage, they thought that HRTs were not needed in TT.

6.4.2.5.2 Concept of <Good learner model>

As I mentioned before, MEXT requests that HRTs perform the role of a good model for learners (Gifu JETs, 2010). Some teachers tried to act as good models for learners, as seen below:

> I do not know how to join in TT. I can learn English the same as children. I wonder that it is OK. (Teacher D, June 5, Interview 1)

> I know that an HRT should be a main teacher in TT. But I am learning English the same as children. (Teacher A, May 27, Interview 1)

Although it is important to act as a good model for learners at this starting point, they were not satisfied with that role.

6.4.2.5.3 Concept of <Demonstration>

The in-service teachers were not satisfied with the role of a good model for learners, shown in the previous concept. They thought that a demonstration for target expressions with an ALT was an HRT's most crucial role, as shown below:

> I am worried about that I should stand in front of children and use English, for example, giving a demonstration for target expressions and showing conversation with the ALT. I have to speak English more. (Teacher A, May 27, Interview 1)

I do not have chances to demonstrate target expressions with the ALT because he can use ICT materials to show target expressions. (Teacher C, May 27, Interview 1)

They were struggling because they wanted to play an active role in TT, but they could not. In their thinking, to improve their English lessons, the top concern was the HRT's role in TT.

6.4.2.6 Category (6) [Assistance]

Category (6) [Assistance] consists of two concepts: <ALTs are needed> and <Manuals are needed>.

6.4.2.6.1 Concept of <ALTs are needed>

The first concept to discuss in this category is <ALTs are needed>. Japanese elementary school teachers wish to work with native speakers (Butler, 2007b) and MEXT encourages teachers to teach with native speakers (MEXT, 2001). The in-service teachers in this study stated the following regarding ALTs:

The ALT speaks all the time. I rarely speak in a lesson. (Teacher C, May 27, Interview 1)

I entrust the ALT with everything about English lessons. (Teacher E, June 5, Interview 1)

Usually I do not have meetings with the ALT. I leave everything to him. (Teacher E, June 5, Interview 1)

Teachers C and E stated that the ALT could teach English by himself without them. Teachers D, E, and F stated that ALTs were needed because they could not teach English by themselves as seen below:

If I teach English by myself, I teach it only in Japanese. (Teacher D, June 5, Interview 1)

I might teach English wrong if I teach by myself. I cannot teach English lessons without ALTs. (Teacher E, June 5, Interview 1)

If the government wants all children to have English competence, it should make a budget to have ALTs or experts at all schools. It is impossible for us amateurs to improve children's communication abilities. Can we do that? (Teacher F, June 24, Interview 1)

At the beginning stages of the study, the teachers showed a heavy reliance on ALTs to teach English. HRTs that work with ALTs have often been observed to be either marginalized in the classroom or overly dependent on ALTs during lessons (Butler, 2007b). One reason for relying so much on ALTs is language proficiency. The teachers with lower English proficiency tend to support the idea that English is best taught by native speakers at the elementary school level (Butler, 2007b). Butler (2007b) added the following:

Elementary school teachers who feel they lack proficiency may not be confident in teaching English to young learners. They therefore may believe that NSs' [native speakers'] communicative competency can compensate for their own lack of proficiency, and may believe that NSs [native speakers] are better suited for the job. (p. 27)

Teachers E and F stated above that HRTs should not teach English because their English competence is not high enough. One of main oppositions to English education in elementary schools is that children might acquire the wrong knowledge and skills if they are taught English by teachers who do not receive enough training (Nishida, 2006). The preference toward including native speakers may be due to the teachers' proficiency levels (Butler, 2007b). The teachers think that they would not be able to teach English by themselves, so they think that ALTs are essential at this stage.

6.4.2.6.2 Concept of <Manuals are needed>

The next concept is <Manuals are needed>. When English lessons were conducted nationally during "the Period for Integrated Studies" without "Eigo Note" or "Hi, friends!" the most critical problem was a lack of tangible guidelines from MEXT. Kusumoto (2008) wrote the following about teachers' conditions at that time:

> Since most teachers do not have a clear idea of the learning objectives and goals, they struggle to decide what to teach and how much to teach it. These problems lead to another challenge, a lack of time and materials. They had to spend tremendous amounts of time on making lesson plans and preparing materials, which creates a heavier work load. (pp. 31-32)

Memories of conducting lessons without any course books, a curriculum, lesson plans, or materials during that time give teachers anxiety. They need a curriculum with detailed lesson plans and materials. This point is confirmed at this stage of the study by the comments below:

> I do not have images of English lessons. Are there any manuals? We need manuals. (Teacher A, May 27, Interview 1)

> It is hard to teach without manuals. We cannot make lesson plans from nothing. We do not have enough knowledge of teaching English. (Teacher B, May 27, Interview 1)

> If ALTs or JTEs (Japanese Teachers of English) prepare everything, it is OK. If we must make a curriculum and materials, it is impossible. (Teacher C, May 27, Interview 1)

> If I have a manual, I can do something. New teachers look at manuals and conduct lessons, don't they? We are the same as them regarding English lessons. (Teacher F, June 24, interview 1)

Teachers A, B, and C stated that they needed manuals, otherwise they could not meet curriculum demands. The teachers were seeking clear instructional manuals with precise procedures (e.g., a curriculum, a course book, lesson plans, and materials). According to Teacher F's comment, even veteran teachers are in the same position as new teachers when it comes to teaching English. This category reveals that the HRTs need ALTs and manuals to conduct English lessons before they participate in lesson study.

6.4.3 Summary of teachers' views on teaching English

The data regarding teachers' views on teaching English showed that the HRTs had negative opinions, although they understood the necessity of English education in the age of internationalization. They worried about creating ideal lessons and were concerned about the HRT's role in TT. However, at this stage, they relied heavily on the ALT because of their low levels of English proficiency and lack of training. In this environment, for their teaching, they believed ALTs and manuals to be essential. After gathering insights from the participants at this stage, the constraints stated above became target areas to help teachers in their development. Reducing their anxiety regarding English competence and playing a productive role in TT were targeted with the aim of improving teacher development. In the next section, I describe three lesson study cycles.

6.5 Descriptions of lesson study cycles in this school

The following documents the lesson study cycles of three teachers (C, D, and E) from the planning stages, through their research lessons, to their post-lesson discussions.

6.5.1 Lesson study 1

Descriptions of lesson study 1 are presented from the planning stage, through the research lesson, to the post-lesson discussion.

6.5.1.1 Planning discussion

Teacher C, who teaches 3rd grade students, was selected to teach the first research lesson because she has experienced teaching English in another city. She developed a lesson plan based on "Hi, friends! 1, Lesson 5" by herself before the planning discussion. She proposed her lesson plan to the faculty during the planning discussion on August 31. I was not invited to the planning discussion. It is usual that a school only invites outside experts to observe a research lesson and make comments in a post-lesson discussion. When I realized, the planning discussion was already finished, and then I asked to be invited to the next planning discussion.

According to the minutes of the proceedings, Teacher C explained her plan by first stating that the main expressions in the lesson were "What color do you like?" and "I like red." This unit had four lessons, and the research lesson was the third one. The main activity was drawing on a T-shirt in pairs, asking each other about favorite colors and shapes. Other teachers were worried about time-keeping because children might become absorbed in drawing, so they gave advice about making rules and time limits. After the other teachers asked some questions about procedures, her plan was accepted.

6.5.1.2 Research lesson

I observed the research lesson on October 7. During the research lesson, the collaborative nature of lesson study was observable, as teachers each took on one role, such as, taking pictures or taking a video. Others who were observers took notes on a sheet on which observation points were written. The lesson started with student monitors saying "Let's start English class." Teacher C stood in front of the classroom with the ALT. After beginning with greetings, she stated "today's goal" and the "activity menu" in Japanese. During the introduction of the target expression, Teacher C took an inductive approach regarding teaching the question phrase "What … do you like?" by asking the phrase "Do you like …?" many times in English to let children realize that a more general strategy is to ask "What … do you like?" In this way, she showed that you do not have to ask "Do you like …?" so many times, as there are other possibilities. During a listening activity, she asked the children "How many pencils?" "How many children?" and "How many cards?" to reinforce this expression for them. These were the vice-principal's ideas to make the children think and to make the lesson more communicative. In a demonstration during the main activity, she answered the ALT's three questions, "What color do you like?" "What shape do you like?" and "How many?" She answered "I like pink." "I like stars." and "Three, please." She gave some instructions and feedback in English during the lesson, such as "Stand up," "Open your textbook to page 20," and "Good job." On the other hand, she also used Japanese, including "*Yubiwo sashitemite* [Point to them]," "*Ima nante itta?* [What did he say?]," "*Mouikkai* [One more time]," "*Yarukoto wakatta?* [Did you understand what to do?]," "*How many? no tsukaikata wakatta?* [Did you understand how to use "How many?"]," "*Moutsukawanaikara tekisutowo shitani oitekudasai* [Put your textbook under your chair because we do not need it anymore]," and so on. The lesson wrapped up with the student monitors saying "Let's finish English class."

6.5.1.3 Post-lesson discussion

The post-lesson discussion on the same day of the research lesson started with the self-evaluation of Teacher C and the ALT. During the post-lesson discussion, teachers shared the roles of facilitator and taking notes on the discussion for the school's official record. The roles rotated each time. Teacher C stated,

> Thank you for coming over to see my lesson. The children were calmer than usual. I focused on the HRT's role today. I tried to use English as much as possible. But I did not understand how much I should be using

Japanese. Sometimes I wondered whether the children understood or not. The children did not understand whether they should say something or if they should repeat after the ALT. My instruction in English was not good. I picked up an expression "How many?" which the children already learned because I would like the children to use English a lot. Thank you. (Teacher C)

The ALT stated in English,

It was a good class. I like 3rd graders. They are easy students [who are motivated with good behavior toward learning English]. The students understood the difference between "Do you like …?" and "What do you like?" It is difficult sometimes. Oh, listening. I was a little surprised that one time, they were OK. Usually, two times or three times listening, then they understand. They understood one time. That was great. Last activity went very well. I wrote three questions, 1-colors, 2-shapes, 3-numbers, on the board. Hopefully they remember "What color?" "What shape?" and "How many?" (ALT)

In the beginning of the post-lesson discussion, the teachers were very quiet. Teachers are often polite and avoid conflict within the group. To avoid conflict and let the group move quickly, they tend to avoid giving opinions and feedback or to reveal their full ability, potentially decreasing the capacity of the group, even if the group comprises knowledgeable teachers (Triwaranyu, 2007). The facilitator (Teacher F) urged Teacher A (a head teacher) to say something.

I am not good at English. I also want to know how much I can use

Japanese. The children in this class tried to listen to English carefully. However, I saw some children could not make a conversation well. I think it was better to show the demonstration and to practice the expressions some more times. (Teacher A)

The children in this class were great. Pronunciation was very good. TT went well. Teacher C stated today's goal and a procedure clearly. (Teacher B)

The relationship with the ALT was very good. It was a good atmosphere. It was nice that Teacher C announced the next activity. (Teacher D)

Teacher C conducted HRT's roles well, classroom control, demonstration with the ALT, announcement of lesson goal and procedure, and so on. (Teacher E)

The teachers discussed that Teacher C's role in TT, especially the announcement of the day's goal, procedures, and the next activities, classroom control, and demonstrations with the ALT were all good. In addition, they decided to ask about the weather, the days of the week, and dates in every lesson in all grades as this school's style. This shows their positive attitude toward teaching English. They wondered how much HRTs should use Japanese. I mentioned that teachers should use English as much as possible, using "classroom English" and repeating the ALT's English. The vice principal, who was an English teacher at the junior high school, mentioned not to translate the ALT's English into Japanese. Then he said the children's pronunciation of words was very good, but their pronunciation of sentences was not good. He requested attention to English rhythm.

Then the teachers talked about their class's children, sometimes mentioning children by name, for example, the 5th grade children fight many times in a lesson, the 1st and 2nd grade children think English lesson as play time, Student-A [4th grade] goes to a cram school for English conversation and he answers every question, and so on. These comments often appear in reflections during the school-based lesson study because all the participants know their school's children very well. They can understand each teacher's situation.

Although an invited outside expert usually does not say anything until the time he/she provides feedback and final comments at the end of discussion, I asked questions and gave some comments during the discussion to activate the conversation. I wanted to think about the lesson from the same points of view as teachers as much as possible.

Through the first lesson study cycle, the teachers observed an English lesson in this school for the first time and gained some insights, shown below:

1. HRTs play the roles of: announcing today's goal, procedures, and the upcoming activities; demonstration with the ALT; and classroom control.

2. Weather-related questions, the days of the week, and the date are asked in every lesson in all grades as this school's style.

3. HRTs should use English as much as possible, using "classroom English" and repeating the ALT's English.

4. The children's pronunciation of English is very good.

5. An MKO can join in the discussion, rather than only giving final evaluative comments.

These insights influenced the later lesson study cycles.

6.5.2 Lesson study 2

Descriptions of lesson study 2 are presented from the planning stage, through the research lesson, to the post-lesson discussion.

6.5.2.1 Planning discussion

Teacher D, who teaches 2nd grade students, was selected to teach the second research lesson. She had never taught English until this year or received any training on teaching English. She made a lesson plan based on this school's original curriculum produced by me. She proposed her lesson plan to the faculty in the planning discussion on October 19. I joined in the planning discussion this time because I wanted to know the teachers' real situations and thinking, and to think together with them about lesson planning to better understand and perhaps share their points of view, instead of just being an outside expert.

Teacher D explained her plan. It was based on a picture book, "Brown Bear, Brown Bear, What Do You See?" This unit had four lessons, and the research lesson was the fourth one. The main activity was drawing a picture showing the children's favorite animals and colors, and then presenting the picture to the class. The other teachers were worried about how the students would handle presenting their pictures. They struggled to give ideas because they did not know the picture book very well. I advised them to divide the students into two groups and have one group ask the questions and the other give the answers. This way, students can say their part rhythmically and the children can help each other as a group. I also introduced how to read the picture book. This planning discussion was conducted without the ALT. One particular change I recommended was to have the ALT in the planning discussion because he can then become familiar with the procedures and know what is important in the unit, which can reduce time needed for later meetings with the ALT.

6.5.2.2 Research lesson

The research lesson was held on October 26, and I observed it. During the research lesson, the teachers each took on one role, as usual. The routine pattern of starting the lesson with student monitors saying "Let's start English class" occurred as in the previous research lesson and ended in the same manner as well, as shown below. This procedure also became part of this school's style. Teacher D stood in front of the classroom with the ALT. When she was asked, "How are you?" by the children, she answered, "I am nervous." After the greetings, she stated "today's goal" and the "activity menu" in both Japanese and English. She used the same cards (weather, days of the week, months) as were used in the previous research lesson, from Teacher C. This is also part of this school's style. During an activity focused on pronunciation of target words and singing a song, Teacher D pronounced and sang along with the children. She was a good learners' model. During the demonstration of how to ask for worksheets, the ALT asked Teacher D, "What animal?" and "What color?" She answered, "Cat, please" and "Green, please." Passing out worksheets and drawings did not go smoothly because the preparation was not good. The teachers should have prepared worksheets and markers for each group ahead of time. When presenting pictures after the drawing, the teacher joined a group and said her parts. In the groups, one half asked the questions and the other half answered. The children helped each other and were able to say their parts rhythmically. During the lesson, the teacher gave some instructions in English, such as, "Change," "Stand up and say," "Green, everyone stand up," "Rock, Scissors, Paper, go," "Just a moment," "What's this?" "Time is up," "Sit down, please," "Here," "Very good." Although she tried to speak only in English, she also used Japanese, for example, "*Yomimasuyo* [I am going to read this]," "*Mite, demonsutoreshon shimasukara* [Look. We are going to show a demonstration]," "*Irowa isshokudake* [You can use only one color]," "*Hitori nimai* [Two sheets for each]," "*Saishonohito* [Who is the first?]," "*Yoninde yaru* [You will do this in groups of four]," "*Mouikkai* [One more time]," "*Gofunde yattekudasai* [You have five minutes to finish]," "*Mihonwo misemasu* [I am going to show a model]," *Yarikata wakatta* [Do you understand how to do it?]," "*Minnanowo matomete ehonni surukarane* [I will put your pictures together and make our original book],"and so on.

6.5.2.3 Post-lesson discussion

The post-lesson discussion on the same day of the research lesson started with the self-evaluation of teacher D and the ALT. During the post-lesson discussion, teachers shared roles, as usual. Teacher D and the ALT stated as below:

> Thank you for coming over to see my lesson. I was worried about whether the children could present their original ideas on their worksheets. I was also worried about how we would demonstrate presenting them. But the children did well. My preparation was not good, especially the issue of the markers being in short supply. So it took a long time to color. I should have been better-prepared for the distribution of the markers and worksheets. The presenting of their pictures finished too quickly. I should have taken more time to enjoy. The children were very calm today. (Teacher D)

We practiced the "Brown Bear, Brown Bear, What Do You See?" book on Friday, and the back-and-forth of questions and answers was pretty well done. I think we should have reviewed a little today so that we would remember and return to the level of last Friday. I think we should have prepared worksheets and markers for each group to avoid confusion. (ALT)

After their comments, the teachers talked about this school's lesson style. Giving name tags to the children at the beginning of a lesson is also one of the routines that is part of this school's English lessons.

The ALT knows the students' names. Is it needed to call names and give name tags? (Teachers F)

The children play with the name tags, so I collected them after calling names. (Teacher D)

It was a good chance to use "Here you are" and "Thank you." (Vice principal)

It is also a good chance for the students to see their own names in the English alphabet. A pinch-type name tag is better to avoid playing. (The author)

The next topic regarded asking the day of the week, the date, and the weather. These questions are difficult for lower-grade children. The teachers agreed to ask these questions every class, with the format depending on the grade level, for example, lower-grade children listen to and repeat the ALT's English but do not answer the questions. The third topic pertained to the announcement of the day's goal.

Teacher D should have mentioned that today's goal was drawing pictures. (Teacher A)

Although I prepared a sample picture, I forgot to show the children. So the children did not understand that today's goal was drawing pictures. (Teacher D)

I added as an MKO:

The children drew the same pictures as the book, the same color and the same animal. They did not change the colors of the animals. They did not understand the meaning of today's main activity. Teacher D should have explained the purpose of drawing pictures showing the children's favorite animals and colors at the beginning. (The author)

In the end of the discussion, I said, "The teachers should have read the picture book, rhythmically and as many times as possible, in the previous lessons, so that the children would remember the phrase patterns of the picture book. It allows the children to remember the original book easily. Repeating rhythmically is useful for lower-grade students." I also suggested that they focus on an English-like pronunciation of "white" and "orange" because the children's pronunciation was similar to Japanese.

In the post-lesson discussion, the teachers discussed the routine of these

English lessons as this school's style. The routine was established. It was a sign of the teachers' motivation to teach English. I was surprised that Teacher D used a lot of English in the lesson. As I mentioned above, she had never taught English or received any training on teaching English. I was impressed with her attitude toward using English as much as possible.

6.5.3 Lesson study 3

Descriptions of lesson study 3 are presented, from the planning stage, through the research lesson, to the post-lesson discussion.

6.5.3.1 Planning discussion

The teacher who took charge of the research lesson for lesson study 3 was Teacher E, who teaches 6th grade students. He had 26 years of teaching experience and four years of experience teaching English. However, the lessons were mainly planned and conducted by the ALT. Teacher E had not planned or taught English lessons by himself. He made a lesson plan based on a course book, "LET'S GO." He proposed his lesson plan to the faculty in the planning discussion on January 20. I was invited to participate in the discussion, but I could not attend because of heavy snow. The ALT could not attend, either. Teacher E explained his plan. The main expressions were "He is my father. He is tall. She is my mother. She is pretty." This unit had four lessons, and the research lesson was the third one. According to the minutes of the proceedings, the vice principal advised having "Who is he?" or "Who is she?" quizzes using famous people, such as President Obama.

6.5.3.2 Research lesson

The research lesson was held on January 26, and I observed it. During the research lesson, the teachers each took on one role, as usual. The lesson began with the student monitors using the English phrases as in the previous research lessons. Teacher E stood in front of the classroom with the ALT. After the greetings, he stated "today's goal" and the "activity menu" in English. He used the same cards (weather, days of the week, the date) as in the previous research lessons of Teachers C and D, as this had become the school's style. To review, Teacher E gave quizzes about famous people using the expressions "Who is he?" and "Who is she?" To work on making sentences, he demonstrated conversation with the ALT. Teacher E did not speak Japanese at all. He cut the last two activities because of the time limit.

6.5.3.3 Post-lesson discussion

The post-lesson discussion on the same day of the research lesson started with the self-evaluation of Teacher E and the ALT. During the post-lesson discussion, the teachers shared roles, as usual. Teacher E and the ALT stated the following:

> I did not have enough time to meet with the ALT before the research lesson because I was busy. The children in my class usually have good communication with the ALT. Today's lesson followed a teacher's manual. It had too many activities, so we could not finish everything. The demonstration of conversation was not good. I think it is not good that students listen to my bad English. (Teacher E)

> I cut two activities. I am sorry about that, but I think that lesson plans in

the teacher's manual are for 60-minute lessons. We should have cut some parts for a 45-minute lessons. (ALT)

First, the teachers stated the following about TT:

Teacher E had a good relationship with the ALT. (Teacher A)

Teacher E helped children who needed help well. (Teacher C)

Teacher E did a good job playing the role of an HRT in TT, with the announcement of "today's goal" and procedures, the demonstration of target expressions with the ALT, and supporting children.

The next topic in the post-lesson discussion regarded writing English. Teacher F asked about teaching letters. Third grade students learn Romanization in Japanese lessons. Children are often confused about Romanization and English. I answered that Romanization was one style of writing Japanese. Teachers should tell children that Romanization is not English to avoid confusion. Teacher A asked, "Can we write in English on the board for long sentences?" I answered "It is OK to write in English for long sentences to help communication. Even if you write in English on the board, you should focus on oral production." MEXT (2007) mentions that "teachers should focus on the foreign language sounds and use letters of the alphabet and words as supplementary tools for oral communication." The teachers began to think of teaching writing English in advance.

The third topic was about quizzes. Teacher E upgraded the activities to include the quizzes, rather than just following the teachers' manual.

"Who is he/she?" was very good because it creates real communication. It was his original activity. (Teacher C)

Teacher E started with President Obama, whom everybody knows, and then continued to unfamiliar people. That was very effective. The children can say "Who is he/she?" naturally. It was better to have more quizzes. (Teacher B)

The vice principal praised some students' pronunciation because they could pronounce the "th" sound in "brother." I commented, "When the children did not answer the ALT's instruction, Teacher E and the ALT did not use Japanese. The ALT explained the same things using different expressions. That was very good. "

In this post-lesson discussion, the teachers also praised Teacher E's role in TT. Teacher E did not speak Japanese at all in the lesson. He conducted the routines and demonstration with the ALT only in English. In addition, he had discussions with the ALT before the research lesson several times. Even if the time was not long, this shows his progress because he had never discussed a lesson with the ALT before.

6.5.4 Summary of the descriptions of lesson study cycles in this school

Three lesson study cycles at the school site were documented in this section. Through the school-based lesson study, I found the following regarding the teachers' development:

1. The teachers established this school's style, which includes that an HRT

announces "today's goal," procedures, and upcoming activities, and asks about the weather, the days of the week, and the date.

2. The teachers reduced their use of Japanese and increased the amount of English use in the lessons.

3. The teachers understood that the children's English pronunciation was very good.

4. The teachers conducted voluntary activities (making reflection cards for the children, having reading time performed by the ALT, teaching the alphabet, making English plates for rooms at school, taking English lessons from the ALT themselves).

The teachers showed progress in teaching English. In the next section, the developmental process of in-service teachers is presented.

6.6 The developmental process of in-service teachers

In this section, I describe collected data and results pertaining to developmental process of in-service teachers associated with their experiences teaching English.

6.6.1 Data collection and analysis

Data collection and analysis were carried out using M-GTA, developed by Kinoshita (2003, 2007) (see Chapter 3, section 3.1). For the *theoretical sampling*, planning and post-lesson discussions and research lessons were electronically recorded for data according to the schedule below (see Table 6.2 in section 6.3).

October 7   Research lesson of Teacher C (45 minutes),

               Post-lesson discussion (90 minutes)

October 19   Planning discussion (90 minutes)

October 26   Research lesson of Teacher D (45 minutes),

               Post-lesson discussion (90 minutes)

January 26   Research lesson of Teacher E (45 minutes),

               Post-lesson discussion (90 minutes)

I also conducted one-on-one and semi-structured interviews per the schedule below. Each was about 60 minutes.

March 10, 2016   Teachers B and D

March 11, 2016   Teachers C and F

March 15, 2016   Teachers A and E

The discussions, research lessons, and interviews were electronically recorded with the consent of the participants. The total recorded time was 855 minutes (14 hours 15 minutes). The minutes of the proceedings and my field notes were also collected for data. In addition, lesson plans for three research lessons and a booklet published at the end of the school year were collected for triangulated data to show qualitative rigor. The data was collected in Japanese and then the analyzed results were translated into English by me.

     First, I developed three concepts based on the minutes of the proceedings, my field notes, and the recorded data from the research lessons, planning discussions, and post-lesson discussions. Those concepts are <HRT's roles in TT>, <Want to learn English more>, and <Classroom English>. After I analyzed the interview data of Teachers B, D, C, and F, I developed two new concepts:

<Learning in the same context> and <Critical views toward ALTs>. Then I analyzed lesson plans for three research lessons and the booklet published at the end of the school year in the same manner. Finally, I analyzed the interview data of Teachers A and E. However, new concepts did not emerge. During the procedure, I developed five concepts.

As stated in Chapter 3, for appropriate validity, as in the case of all the studies in this research, I asked my co-worker to develop concepts from the transcripts as peer-debriefing. She came up with four concepts: <HRT's roles in TT>, <Classroom English>, <Applying pedagogical knowledge>, and <Want to teach by oneself>. Two of our concepts were the same, while the other two were different, so we discussed which were better. In addition, we checked frequent words and co-occurrence networks using KH Coder Ver.2 (see Appendices 8 & 9). Then I added <Applying pedagogical knowledge> and <Want to teach by oneself>, and kept the other concepts. We decided on seven concepts at this stage (Open coding, see Chapter 3, section 3.2). In the next step, I created categories and labeled them using [ ] symbols (Selective coding). Several concepts were integrated into each category. I showed the concepts and categories to my co-worker. We then confirmed that we could come up with no more new concepts or categories, determining that we had reached *theoretical saturation.*

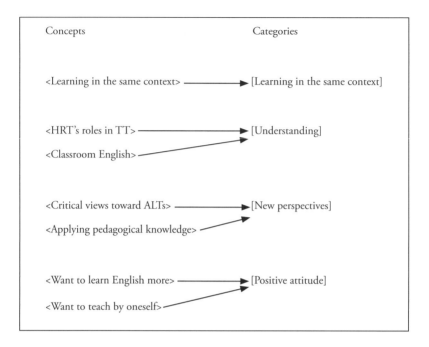

Finally, I made a diagram and a storyline and showed them to my co-worker. She agreed with my interpretations (see Figure 6.3).

6.6.2 Results and discussion

All categories and concepts are summarized in the diagram (Figure 6.3). The diagram shows four categories: (1) [Learning in the same context], (2) [Understanding], (3) [New perspectives], and (4) [Positive attitude].

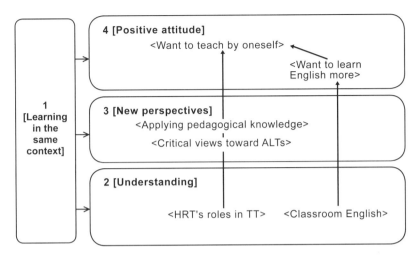

Figure 6.3. The developmental process of in-service teachers

> **Storyline**
> The teachers developed in [Leaning in the same context]. The teachers' [Understanding] of <HRT's roles in TT> and <Classroom English> improved. [New perspectives] of <Critical views toward ALTs> and <Applying pedagogical knowledge> then occurred. Finally, the teachers began to <Want to learn English more> and <Want to teach by oneself> in [Positive attitude].

6.6.2.1 Category (1) [Learning in the same context]

Although prefecture- or government-mandated seminars and one-time workshops conducted by outside experts in a top-down approach, are available in Japan, its real impact is limited because teachers may find that some of the ideas presented are often far different in practice from the reality of their classrooms (Farrell, 2007). On the other hand, study outcomes have shown that school-based lesson study is efficient because teachers can learn in the same context as that in which they teach. Teachers' comments correspond with this concept, as seen below:

I cannot adapt things which were given outside my class, even though it is very good. When I attend a seminar, I always listen to other people's affairs. School-based lesson study is very good because we can adjust discussions to our situations. We can struggle many times and learn practically. If I learn by myself, I might not do my best. I think that this school has a learning environment. That is good for me. (Teacher C, March 11, Interview 2)

If I go to a seminar or see the lesson study of another school, I cannot sympathize with the lesson because it is conducted for children whom I do not know. However, I know the situation of the teachers and children in school-based lesson study. Thinking and watching lessons, and exchanging ideas in my school were very useful for me. (Teacher A, March 15, Interview 2)

Lewis and Hurd (2011) stated that "one-size-fits-all professional development rarely meets the needs of all teachers within a school or district" (p. 7). Traditional expert-led workshops are disconnected from real classrooms. Further teacher comments support this claim.

It was effective to watch other teachers' lessons. It is valuable that we can see children that we all know. And we could exchange ideas considering the children's situations. (Teacher B, March 10, Interview 2)

Young teachers have no experiences to think and create lessons by themselves. They are instructed by administrators or supervisors in a top-down manner and conduct lessons without thinking themselves. When I was young, enough time was guaranteed at each school for teachers to think and prepare their lessons. The lesson study we conducted this year was very good because we could put our heads together in the same situation. Teacher C and Teacher D, who were young, could think without believing all of the other teachers' advice based simply on trust. (Teacher F, March 11, Interview 2)

I discussed problems and worries with other teachers facing the same situation as me. Previously, I thought that I was the only teacher who struggled with English education. Exchanging conversations about problems and worries made me feel at ease. (Teacher D, March 10, Interview 2)

The in-service teachers observed lessons together and could learn from the reality of their classrooms. Professional development must be situated in the familiar context of the teachers' own teaching for them to make sense of theory (Johnson, 1996). Colleagues can understand each other's situations and provide appropriate suggestions for specific situations. In addition, as Teacher D stated, collaboration also helps to reduce anxiety and isolation among teachers.

6.6.2.2 Category (2) [Understanding]

Before the lesson study, the categories [Want to learn HRT's roles in TT] and [Anxiety] emerged. The in-service teachers felt anxiety about teaching English because of their lack of English competence. They wanted to learn the HRT's roles in TT as the first step in teacher development. After they experienced school-based lesson study, category (2) [Understanding] emerged, which consists of two concepts, <HRT's roles in TT> and <Classroom English>.

6.6.2.2.1 Concept of <HRT's roles in TT>

The teachers in the study used to rely heavily on ALTs to conduct lessons and had previously just observed lessons, rather than teaching them. However, the teachers whose comments are provided below changed their attitudes, playing HRTs' roles in the lessons.

> At the beginning of this year, the ALT led a lesson alone, and I just observed that. Now I am ready to take an HRT's role. I learned how to lead an English lesson in TT. (Teacher A, March 15, Interview 2)

> I conducted demonstrations of target expressions with the ALT and announced the next activity during the lesson. (Teacher B, March 10, Interview 2)

> I go to the front when I am called for demonstrations. Conversations with the ALT are getting more and more frequent. I try to speak English as much as I can. (Teacher A, March 15, Interview 2)

HRTs who work with ALTs have often been observed to be either marginalized in the classroom or overly dependent on ALTs during lessons (Butler, 2007b). However, the teachers above played an HRT's roles during the lessons, for example, demonstrations of target expressions with the ALT.

> I made announcements about starting and closing and about the day's goal and activity menu because we decided that these are our routines.

(Teacher F, March 11, Interview 2)

We could standardize the HRT's roles. (Teacher A, March 15, Interview 2)

The teachers standardized the HRT's roles (greetings and closing, announcement of the day's goal, activity menu, the next activity, and asking about the weather, days of the week, and the date) on their own initiative. The teachers called these roles this school's style. This demonstrates their positive attitude toward teaching English in TT.

6.6.2.2.2 Concept of <Classroom English>

Machida (2016) stated that it is necessary to reduce the pressure on elementary school teachers regarding the perceived necessity of speaking like native English speakers. These teachers became accustomed to speaking English, as indicated in their comments below:

During this year, I became familiar with English, (Teacher B, March 10, Interview 2)

I began to come to the front in the classroom and use some English. (Teacher F, March 11, Interview 2)

I became familiar with English. I talk to the ALT as much as I can. (Teacher E, March 15, Interview 2)

Although I found English lessons difficult the first time, I became accustomed. I remembered a lot of English by repeating English after the ALT during the lessons. (Teacher A, March 15, Interview 2)

Not many English words are needed for teaching English. I often repeated English after the ALT, and then I would remember many standard expressions. (Teacher C, March 11, Interview 2)

I have learned the pronunciation difference between "bug" and "bag" along with the children. I realized that even simple English for example "Chairs, back," was understandable. I became familiar with listening. I would like to use English as much as I can. (Teacher E, March 11, Interview 2)

I have learned the pronunciation difference between "Lice" and "Rice." Through listening to the ALT's explanation, I learned it along with the children. (Teacher A, March 15, Interview 2)

The teachers learned English from the ALT along with the children as learners during TT. They understood that simple English was understandable and not many English words were needed to teach English in elementary schools.

6.6.2.3 Category (3) [New perspectives]

The category (3) [New perspectives] consists of two concepts, <Critical views toward ALTs> and <Applying pedagogical knowledge>. Before lesson study, the category [ALTs are needed] emerged. The in-service teachers thought that they could not teach English by themselves because of their lack of English competence, so they believed ALTs were essential. However, the teachers' thinking has changed over the course of their school-base lesson study. The teachers no longer rely on the ALT blindly. They began to see the ALT's value through their own sharpened teachers' eyes.

6.6.2.3.1 Concept of <Critical views toward ALTs>

The teachers' points of view toward the ALTs changed. They began complaining that the ALT did not give the children enough time to listen and think. The teachers' comments are provided below:

> I want the ALT to talk a lot in English with the children at lunch time, but he does not. He is kind, calm, and a very good person, but he rarely talks to the children outside of the lessons. I would like him to lead conversations with the children at lunch time. (Teacher A, March 15, Interview 2)

The teachers thought that communication with ALTs was very good for children. They wanted the ALTs to talk to the children more. More comments from the teachers are below:

> The ALT speaks English too slowly sometimes. I would like him to speak naturally. He often gives answers to the children quickly. I want the children to think well, so I would like him to take some time. (Teacher C, March 11, Interview 2)

> The ALT moved to output activities quickly, but the children cannot perform output activities well without enough input. (Teacher E, March 15, Interview 2)

I would like to give hints to help the children think well. The ALT does not have time to think. I began to think that the ALT was not an educator, and only an English native speaker. (Teacher B, March 10, Interview 2)

The teachers thought that listening to a lot of English was important for children. They complained that the ALT was not giving the children enough time to listen and think, giving answers too quickly or requesting output from them.

I think that classroom control and making a unit topic attractive are the HRT's job. We do those things in other subjects, such as math, science, and social studies. An ALT is only a native speaker, not an elementary school teacher. (Teacher B, March 10, Interview 2)

I began to think that I do not want to believe in an ALT too much. I would like to see ALTs critically. I am going to request anything to make lessons better for the children. (Teacher E, March 15, Interview 2)

The ALT does not know the children individually very well, so HRTs should monitor the process of lessons and sometimes make requests to ALTs. (Teacher F, March 11, Interview 2)

I came to think that an HRT's job was to observe the children carefully and request the ALT to teach according to the children's situation, and to create natural situations in which to use target expressions. My thinking changed after the research lesson. (Teacher E, March 15, Interview 2)

The teachers realized that ALTs were only native speakers of English, and not teachers. In fact, many ALTs are not certified teachers in their own countries. Some do not have any formal educational training, and some have little knowledge of the English language structure (Tajino & Tajino, 2000). As experienced teachers, the teachers can observe their children very carefully and think of ways to make lessons attractive in other subjects. They have the ability to evaluate good lessons. They gained the confidence to see English lessons through teachers' eyes, as they do with other subjects. Teacher E stated that he did not want to rely on ALTs too much. The teachers began to see ALTs critically, and their points of view toward ALTs changed. It can be said that the teachers became autonomous regarding teaching English.

6.6.2.3.2 Concept of <Applying pedagogical knowledge>

The teachers realized that an HRT's job was to observe the children carefully and teach based on the children's needs. The teachers' comments are provided below:

> I found that Teacher D observed the children carefully. I began to think that HRTs can create good lessons even for English lessons. (Teacher F, October 26, post-lesson discussion)

> Teacher E started with quizzes including President Obama, whom everybody knows, and then continued to name unfamiliar people. I was impressed with this idea. HRTs can also make activities interesting in English lessons. (Teacher C, January 26, post-lesson discussion)

I think that classroom control and making a unit topic attractive are the HRT's job. We do those things in other subjects, such as math, science, and social studies. (Teacher B, March 10, Interview 2)

Why don't we put signs of procedures on the board? The children can see the perspective of a lesson. (Teacher F, October 7, post-lesson discussion)

Teachers can be considered to already have pedagogical knowledge in other subjects, and their knowledge and skills can be applied to English teaching. The teachers realized that they could observe their children very carefully and make lessons attractive in a way similar to other subjects.

6.6.2.4 Category (4) [Positive attitude]

The category (4) [Positive attitude] consists of two concepts, <Want to learn English more> and <Want to teach by oneself>. Before lesson study, the category [Really needed?] emerged. The in-service teachers were opposed to teaching English at elementary schools. However, the teachers became more positive through their school-base lesson study.

6.6.2.4.1 Concept of <Want to learn English more>

A positive attitude toward using English in the classroom could be seen during the research lessons. During the first research lesson, Teacher C used a lot of Japanese. In the second research lesson, Teacher D reduced the amount of Japanese use and increased the amount of English use. In the third research lesson, Teacher E did not use any Japanese. Through their school-based lesson study, the teachers became more positive regarding the progress of their English ability. The in-service teachers mentioned that they would like to learn and practice English more, as seen below:

> I would like to practice to progress in my English skills. This is needed to demonstrate with the ALT during lessons. It was usually pointed out that my English pronunciation and accent were wrong by the ALT when I repeated after him. I began to use more English than before. (Teacher B, March 10, Interview 2)

> I began to think that I want to speak English. If I do, I will be able to give good English lessons. (Teacher F, March 11, Interview 2)

> Although I am not good at using English yet, I am getting better. I would like to use English more practically. (Teacher D, March 10, Interview 2)

The teachers took classroom English lessons once a week during the school-based lesson study, as indicated in their comments below:

> We all have motivation, and we have started to practice classroom English, which consists of formulaic expressions teachers use in the classroom. That was very good. (Teacher B, March 10, Interview 2)

> It was effective that we took classroom English lessons. The ALT, and at times the vice principal, were instructors. (Teacher D, March 10, Interview 2)

It was good to have classroom English lessons each time we had discussions. (Teacher C, March 11, Interview 2)

I think it was good to have classroom English lessons once a week. We all enjoyed it. (Teacher B, March 10, Interview 2)

Furthermore, they wanted to become competent in using English flexibly, as indicated in their comments below:

I particularly want to learn the English used in "Hi, friends!" [supplemental books distributed to pupils by MEXT] perfectly, as well as classroom English. I would like to learn them as patterns and then apply them in context. (Teacher F, March 11, Interview 2)

I would like to use English appropriately, based on the situation. (Teacher C, March 11, Interview 2)

I would like to be able to speak English more. I would like to use phrases in appropriate situations. (Teacher A, March 15, Interview 2)

The teachers became more positive about improving their English ability.

6.6.2.4.2 Concept of <Want to teach by oneself>

The teachers below mentioned that they would like to be able to lead English lessons.

I need to have more teaching skills. (Teacher D, March 10, Interview 2)

HRTs in K city strongly perpetrate their roles and control the ALT. When I observed a research lesson in Y school, the HRT was the main teacher and conducted the lesson entirely in English. He spoke more English than an ALT. He looked confident. I would like to lead a lesson and praise children in English based on the circumstances. (Teacher A, March 15, Interview 2)

I conducted an English lesson in an open class for parents. I did not imagine that I could conduct an English lesson in an open class one year ago. The parents were very interested in the English lesson and were pleased to see it. (Teacher C, March 11, Interview 2)

We requested students who were learning English at university to teach English lessons in our class last year without meeting with them first. Thinking back now, it was terrible to leave classes up to university students, not teachers. Now I think I should control lessons myself because those are my classes. (Teacher B, March 10, Interview 2)

I left everything to the ALT and university students last year, but I became more positive toward English lessons this year. (Teacher C, March 11, Interview 2)

Surprisingly, university students, rather than the teachers, taught English lessons in these classes in previous years. This was because they thought that university students had strong English abilities than them. However, the teachers changed their minds about teaching English themselves during their school-based lesson study. The teachers also became ready to upgrade English to an official subject, in which they would teach not only listening and speaking but also reading and writing, as seen below:

> I think that HRTs should teach the alphabet and some parts of phonics in the near future. (Teacher C, March 11, Interview 2)

> After English becomes a subject in 2020, I need more specific knowledge of teaching English, especially reading and writing. (Teacher A, March 15, Interview 2)

> After English becomes a subject in 2020, the number of lessons will increase and the instructing of reading and writing letters will start. We have to learn more about teaching English. (Teacher F, March 11, Interview 2)

The teachers became more confident and began to consider being able to teach English by themselves, without ALTs, as indicated in their comments below:

> I would like to think about lessons, materials, procedures, and questions by myself with the aim to conduct English lessons alone in the near future. (Teacher B, March 10, Interview 2)

> The next step is teaching by ourselves without ALTs. I would like to engage more significantly in my roles. (Teacher C, March 11, Interview 2)

Gardner and Leak (1994) mentioned that "anxiety lessens with teaching experience" (p. 30). Morton, Vesco, Williams, and Awender (1997) stated that "teaching itself appears to be one viable intervention strategy to reduce anxiety" (p. 76). It can be said that the more teaching experience teachers have, the less anxiety they feel. Most researchers have concluded that teacher development focusing on realistic areas of teaching reduces anxiety among teachers. The teachers in this study do not rely on ALTs heavily anymore. Their outcomes indicate an increased positive attitude as teachers.

6.6.3 Summary of the developmental process of in-service teachers

The developmental process of the in-service teachers had three stages: [Understanding], [New perspectives], and [Positive attitude] in [Learning in the same context]. They realized the value of learning in the same context as that in which they teach. First, they began to understand the HRT's roles in TT and classroom English. Second, they changed their point of view toward ALTs and realized that they could apply their pedagogical knowledge to teaching English. Third, they had a more positive attitude toward learning English and toward teaching English by themselves.

6.7 Summary of chapter

In this chapter, a study on in-service teachers was presented. First, the teachers' views concerned with teaching English in elementary schools were presented. Then I described three lesson study cycles. Finally, the developmental process of the in-service teachers associated with their experiences teaching English was presented. The in-service teachers had negative thoughts toward teaching English in elementary schools. During their school-based lesson study, they changed their thinking and became more positive toward teaching English. In the next chapter, I discuss the results from Chapter 4 and Chapter 6.

Chapter 7

Discussion

This study investigated the developmental process of elementary school teachers associated with their experiences teaching English during lesson study. In this chapter, the research questions set at the beginning of the study are addressed. The first area of discussion looks at the results regarding the pre-service teachers, followed by the questions pertaining to the in-service teachers. Then, additional findings from the study are addressed. In Chapter 1, three research questions were posed:

1. How do pre-service teachers develop in terms of teaching English over the course of their teaching practicums while engaged in lesson study?
2. How do in-service teachers view the inclusion of English in the national curriculum?
3. How do in-service teachers develop in terms of teaching English during school-based lesson study?

These questions are addressed in this chapter according to the findings in the preceding chapters (see Chapters 4 & 6). The following discussions are based on the conceptualizations of the teachers' developmental process that were depicted in Figure 4.1 and Figure 6.3.

7.1 Developmental process of pre-service teachers (research question 1)

Research question 1 focused on the developmental process of pre-service teachers. This question is addressed through the analysis in Chapter 4 (see Figure 4.1). The outcomes showed that the pre-service teachers' learning changed along with their development, from "Learning in an authentic classroom" to "Realizing their shortage of knowledge and skills" and "Development in collegiality." They gained a better understanding of (1) [Children's ways of learning English], (2) [English knowledge], (3) [Instructional knowledge], (4) [Importance of English use], (5) [Purpose of Foreign Language Activities], and (6) [Collegiality] during their teaching practicums. The pre-service teachers in this study were better able to learn by observing children, planning and conducting lessons jointly and discussing their experiences and ideas with peers. The pre-service teachers reduced their anxiety of teaching and became more positive.

In particular, the participants showed professional gains in important areas of teaching. In a highly cited paper on teacher knowledge, Shulman (1987) first set up two major dimensions: pedagogical knowledge (PK, knowledge of how to teach) and content knowledge (CK, knowledge of the subject matter, that is, syntactic and semantic aspects of English). He then merged these two necessary understandings of teaching to form what he referred to as pedagogical content knowledge (PCK). He mentioned "the blending of content and pedagogy into an understanding of how particular topics, problems, or issues are organized, represented, and adapted to the diverse interests and abilities of learners, and presented for instruction" (p. 8). He believed that teacher education programs should combine the two knowledge fields. Thus, teachers' PK and CK were being treated as mutually necessary dimensions of professional knowledge that teachers should possess or aim for in their teacher development. Figure 7.1 shows the relationship of PCK (how to teach the subject) with PK (how to teach) and CK (what to teach). The intersection of the two connecting circles represents PCK as the interplay between pedagogy and content. PCK is the concept of formulating the subject such that it is made comprehensible to others (Shulman, 1986).

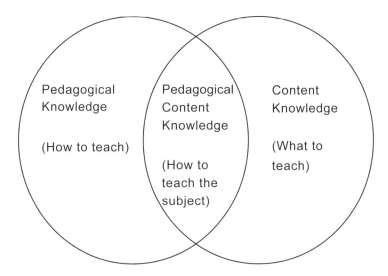

Figure 7.1. The relationship among pedagogical content knowledge, pedagogical knowledge, and content knowledge. The intersection of the two connecting circles represents pedagogical content knowledge.

The pre-service teachers learned PK, as seen in category (3) [Instructional knowledge], in practice. In my own experience of teaching all subjects in elementary school (including English) for more than 20 years, I can attest to the claim that these identified areas of PK are needed in all subjects when individuals become elementary school teachers. The pre-service teachers learned <Flexibility>, <Time control>, and <Understanding children's situations>. They also learned CK, as shown in category (2) [English knowledge]. They learned basic and familiar English words and practical expressions that they did not learn in their junior high and high school days. In addition, they learned PCK in category (4) [Importance of English use] in order to teach English effectively. Unlike the in-service teachers, the pre-service teachers were not well-developed in PK, let alone CK and PCK. The outcome shows that pre-service teachers learn PK, CK, and PCK simultaneously during their teaching practicums. They are, in a sense, empty vessels to fill due to their lack of experience and developmental maturity.

The outstanding outcomes among the pre-service teachers are further addressed here. Concerning category (1) [Children's ways of learning English], observing children's ways of learning English can have a significant impact on the development of pre-service teachers. These teachers realized that children learn English in different ways from them. The pre-service teachers learned English through a traditional method that used direct deductive explanations of grammar and translations. However, they understood that children can learn English inductively, without explanations or translations. They also understood that authentic communication was important, not just fun games and songs. Consequently, they no longer believed that the alphabet and grammar should be taught first, or that only songs and games were used in English lessons. Learning in a real classroom, rather than a simulated one, has an impact on pre-service teachers. This effect is even more significant regarding English lessons than lessons in other subjects because these participants-and many pre-service teachers like them across Japan-had never observed English lessons in elementary schools, as English lessons were not part of the elementary school curriculum when they attended.

Concerning category (6) [Collegiality], this study suggests that peer learning is very useful in the teaching practicum. Cohan and Honigsfeld (2007) have previously found "that collaboration and dialogues about teaching greatly benefit pre-service teachers" (p. 87). The pre-service teachers deepened their knowledge of teaching and were able to constructively reflect on what they were doing using their peers' advice. They were also able to discuss worries and anxiety with someone in the same position, which could help reduce their anxiety where concerns teaching. Although the HRT has a lot of experience and plays an important role as an MKO by giving advice to the pre-service teachers, she cannot think as a novice teacher. Collegiality was a key experience for pre-service teachers.

7.2 In-service teachers' views on teaching English (research question 2)

Research question 2 addressed the in-service teachers' views on the inclusion of English in the national curriculum (see Chapter 6, section 6.4). Figure 6.2 shows the in-service teachers' views as two core-categories as: "Objection" and "Implementation."

The view that I discuss first is the core-category "Objection". The in-service teachers in this study had negative opinions about teaching English in elementary schools before lesson study. The main reasons are below:

- Japanese language education is more important than English education.
- New problems in education, such as special needs education and a decline in Japanese and academic ability, are more important than

English education.

- Elementary school teachers are busy teaching other subjects.
- The policy came in a top-down manner without reflecting teachers' realities in their local school settings.
- HRTs feel anxiety because their English competence is not high enough and they have not received the proper training to teach English.

This outcome supports the results of another study showing that 78.9% of elementary school HRTs felt that conducting an English activity was a big burden and nearly one-third of the participants thought that English was not needed at the elementary school level (Kusumoto, 2008). Elementary school teachers feel overloaded because they teach all subjects all day without spare time. In addition, most of the elementary school teachers did not learn how to teach English at university, and there are many teachers who have not had enough training in teaching English. The teachers in this study felt anxiety because teaching English was completely new to them. This outcome corresponds with reported teacher anxiety in the literature review (see Chapter 2, section 2.2.4).

The second view that I discuss is the core-category "Implementation". Although the in-service teachers in this study opposed English education in elementary schools, they also thought that teaching English was a necessity because of internationalization. They had clear images of ideal lessons in which children learn practical English through communication and with joy, in comparison to the traditional English education through which the in-service teachers learned. For their development, they thought that the first step was to understand an HRT's roles in TT. However, the teachers showed a heavy reliance on ALTs to teach English, which related to their lack of English proficiency at this stage. In addition, the teachers were also seeking clear instructional manuals (e.g., a curriculum, a course book, lesson plans, and materials). The in-service teachers needed ALTs and manuals to start their English lessons. They were conflicted between objection and implementation.

7.3 Developmental process of in-service teachers (research question 3)

In research question 3, the developmental process of in-service teachers (see Chapter 6, section 6.6) was analyzed. Figure 6.3 shows the process. The in-service teachers in this study developed in three stages, [Understanding], [New perspectives], and [Positive attitude] in [Leaning in the same context], during the school-based lesson study.

The teachers developed in two main areas: attitudes toward the HRT's roles and the use of English in the classroom. Regarding the HRT's roles, the teachers discussed these roles in TT and then decided on standardized HRT roles (greetings and closing, announcement of the day's goal, announcement of the activity menu, announcing the next activity, and asking about the weather, days of the week, and the date). They became familiar with acting out their roles during TT. Finally, they began to want to teach English by themselves, without ALTs.

Regarding using English, first they learned classroom English, that is, standard expressions to be used in English classrooms. They repeated these after the ALT during class and memorized useful expressions. In addition, they began taking English lessons for themselves. The amount of English they used in the classroom setting increased. Finally, they decided they wanted to learn more English, and to develop the flexibility to use English based on the children's situations. They thought that having flexibility in using English was needed to teach English lessons by themselves, without the help of ALTs.

The teachers changed their way of thinking about teaching and became more positive about learning. The teachers' realization that they could apply their PK of other subjects to English was a key point. In post-lesson discussions, they realized that they as HRTs could observe the children carefully and make lessons more attractive. They gained confidence in evaluating good English lessons through teachers' eyes. The teachers reduced their reliance on the ALT and became more positive toward the idea of teaching English lessons by themselves, without ALTs.

7.4 In-service teachers compared with pre-service teachers

As previously stated, pre-service teachers learn PK, CK, and PCK simultaneously during their teaching practicums. On the other hand, although CK and PCK of English education are new to in-service teachers, they already have PK in their teaching experiences of other subjects and can apply that PK to teaching English. Machida (2016) mentioned that "teachers might have learned how to develop their own pedagogical approaches to teaching unfamiliar subjects through their working experience" (p. 58). In-service teachers already know that understanding children is essential to creating lessons and being able to assess good lessons. Realizing this gives them confidence to create English lessons.

Lesson study is based on the reasoning that teaching is a complex activity, and that the best way to learn how to improve instruction is to address it within an authentic classroom context (Howey & Zimpler, 1994; Johnson, Ratsoy, Holdaway, & Friesen, 1993). Both pre-service and in-service teachers had collaborative lesson study and realized that learning in the same context as that in which they teach is highly effective. For pre-service teachers, collaborative lesson study provides them the opportunity to build professional learning communities and develop habits of critical observation, analysis, and feedback (Chokshi & Fernandez, 2004). The pre-service teachers in this study deepened their knowledge and reduced their anxiety toward teaching English. The benefits of lesson study will transfer to their own classrooms in the future (Carrier, 2011). The in-service teachers realized that teachers could learn in the same context as that in which they teach during their school-based lesson study. Colleagues can understand other teachers' situations and give appropriate advice. In addition, exchanging problems and worries with someone in the same position made them feel at ease. Learning in the same context not only adds to knowledge gain, but also provides emotional support. Al-Weher (2004), Graham et al. (1997), and Gunstone et al. (1993) concluded that peer discussions, collaborative group activities, and strong personal and professional relationships were critical elements for effective teacher development.

Regarding ALTs, the pre-service teachers did not want to teach with ALTs in TT because they did not think that they could communicate with the ALTs. They did not know how effective TT with ALTs could be. One the other hand, ALTs were essential for in-service teachers. This study showed that TT with ALTs played a crucial role in all teachers' development associated with teaching English. This is discussed later.

7.5 Additional findings from this study

I describe additional findings from this study: "MKO" and "TT with ALTs."

7.5.1 MKO

The role of an MKO is hugely important throughout the lesson study process (Cohan & Honigsfed, 2007). However, Japan is usually associated with the hierarchical apprenticeship model commonly seen in Confucian cultures (see Chapter 2, section 2.3.3). An outside advisor is usually invited only to key meetings (Fernandez, 2002). The presence of older or more experienced teachers sometimes put limitations on collaborative dialog. In my own experiences over the years of participating in numerous post-lesson discussions, I can attest to the observation that an MKO usually provides final comments at the end of a post-lesson discussion, often speaking for upward of 30 minutes. Teachers do not have the chance to ask questions of the MKO or to discuss among the group. Questioning an authority may be interpreted as challenging or showing disrespect to that authority (Arnold, 1999). Teachers are expected to respect and obey their teaching authority in order to maintain the hierarchy and harmony.

However, careful attention to mutual trust is the key to supporting teachers. To refine lesson study in Japan in a collaborative manner, I think that an MKO's roles should be refined. At the beginning of this study, when I began to discuss teaching with the teachers as an MKO, they did not smile at all and had stern expressions. I made voluntary visits twelve times over the course of the whole year because I wanted to interact with teachers by trying to be in the same position as them as much as possible. The visits allowed me to gain a better understanding of this school's teachers and the children's situations. Knowing the school context informed the MKO to give more appropriate advice. Consequently, as rapport progressively became established, teachers smiled and became relaxed around me.

In spite of the long history of lesson study in Japan, there is no clearly defined professional development system for an MKO (Wang-Iverson & Yoshida, 2005). Researchers outside Japan have investigated an MKO's roles in lesson study. The roles of an MKO are to raise questions, add new perspectives, and be a co-researcher, without telling others what to do (Lewis & Hurd, 2011). MKOs should not aggressively prescribe solutions or attempt to fix the lesson. They can share their expertise or professional knowledge and encourage teachers to keep moving forward. They should pay attention to the teachers and anticipate what they are ready to learn. An MKO's role is not to instruct the teachers or manage their work. The relationship is not hierarchical. Moreover, it is important for MKOs to have spent time and have some rapport with teachers. They should not be seen as one-time visitors. The effective programs tend to be conducted with frequent feedback and follow-up. Outside experts who do not know the personal needs of students and teachers, the community, or the district espouse their own knowledge and discrete skills to improve individual practices (Dobbs, 2000). Long-term, site-based professional development built from teachers' current knowledge and practices is needed (Takahashi, 2014).

7.5.2 TT with ALTs

Having an ALT was particularly effective in the beginning of the teachers' development. Most elementary school teachers cannot start teaching English by themselves because they have not had proper training regarding teaching English and do not have high-enough English competence. In TT, the teachers were able to observe how English lessons progressed (content, activities, and so on) and gain a better understanding of an HRT's roles. They were also able to learn English from the ALT. They repeated after the ALT in TT, and they took classroom English lessons taught by the ALT. The extent of the HRTs' roles and their use of English during TT increased with time. They then compared their ideal teaching method with the ALT's teaching method. The teachers gradually reduced their reliance on the ALT and considered teaching on their own without ALT assistance.

7.6 Summary of chapter

In this chapter, the answers to three research questions were addressed. Then a comparative analysis was carried out discussing commonalities and differences between in-service teachers and pre-service teachers. Finally, additional findings from the study were discussed. In the next chapter, the conclusion of the study is given.

Chapter 8

Conclusion

In this conclusion chapter, a summary of the study is presented. Then, theoretical implications, pedagogical implications, contributions of the study, limitations, and directions for future study follow. Finally, a concluding statement is given.

8.1 Summary of the study

This study focused on the developmental process of elementary school teachers associated with teaching English in lesson study. Teaching English in elementary schools is a new concept in the national curriculum of Japan and is taught mostly by HRTs, who have not had proper training regarding English language instruction. Teacher development is an urgent matter. However, because of a lack of research, elementary school teachers' actual situations are not clear. Therefore, this study investigated the situational realities of teachers in order to document their developmental process.

The data collection was largely based on discussions during lesson study and interviews. The data analysis was based on methods applied using M-GTA (Kinoshita, 2003, 2007). That is, the findings were conceptualized into core-categories, categories, and supporting concepts.

This study first depicted the developmental process of pre-service teachers in Chapter 4 (see Figure 4.1). In contrast to in-service teachers, the outcomes show that pre-service teachers learn PK, CK, and PCK simultaneously during their teaching practicums. The pre-service teachers realized that children learn English inductively without explanations or translations. Learning in a real classroom environment had an impact on pre-service teachers. They changed their beliefs. The impact was pedagogically larger than that in other subjects because the teachers had never observed English lessons in an elementary school. Through collaborative lesson study, they deepened their knowledge and reduced their anxiety. Ultimately, they became more positive toward teaching English.

In-service teachers in this study had negative opinions about teaching English in elementary schools. They felt anxiety because they had not had proper training regarding teaching English and did not have enough English competence. To start English lessons, their first step was to understand an HRT's roles in TT. In Chapter 6, a representational model of their developmental process was shown (see Figure 6.3). Learning in the same context as that in which they teach had a significant impact on their teacher development. Colleagues can understand each other's situations and give appropriate advice, which reduces their anxiety. After the in-service teachers understood the HRT's roles in TT, they began to take more of an active role in their own TTs. They realized that they could apply their PK of other subjects to English. They gained confidence and began to think they could teach English by themselves, without ALTs. They became more positive toward learning more about English. Teachers often resist change mandated or suggested by others, but they do engage in change that they initiate, in what Richardson (1994) calls *voluntary change*. They undertake change voluntarily, following their sense of what their students need and what is working. Collaborative lesson study may lead to the voluntary process.

8.2 Theoretical implications

Theorizing is an important component of M-GTA. In this study, I investigated and theorized regarding the developmental process of elementary school teachers associated with teaching English in lesson study for the first time in the research field. Figure 4.1 showed the developmental process of pre-service teachers and Figure 6.3 showed the developmental process of in-service teachers. The M-GTA focuses on organizing substantive theory for practical utilization (Kinoshita, 1999, 2003). I assume that persons engaged in practical use of the theory are teacher educators who plan teacher development.

8.3 Pedagogical implications

Responding to the recent drastic change in English education at the elementary school level in Japan, each school and the school board of each region need to be aware of teachers' thinking and their developmental process. Understanding their particular concerns is necessary to helping them make changes in their instruction.

Based on the outcomes of "Learning in the same context," it can be recommended that each regional school board should promote on-going school-based lesson study regarding teaching English, not just one-shot seminars. Concerning pre-service teachers, the outcomes of this study suggest that schools should consider giving pre-service teachers more opportunities to learn about teaching English in real classrooms and that they should strongly recommend teachers create one lesson unit together and conduct it collaboratively. Participation in the teaching practicum is the only chance to learn practically during their university days (Sasajima, 2009).

"TT with ALTs" is a crucial part of teacher development as it pertains to teaching English. During TT, teachers can see and imitate an ALT's lessons. Then the extent of the HRT's roles and their use of English during TT increases. Ultimately, as the participants in this study showed, they begin to feel that they would like to teach English by themselves, without ALTs. This outcome suggests that the school board should assign an ALT to each school as often as possible or, at a minimum, prioritize schools in which teachers are not familiar with teaching English.

8.4 Contributions of the study

This study contributed to the body of research in the area of teacher development. It may help administrators understand teachers' developmental process and plan effective teacher development. This study contributed specifically in the following ways:

- This study focused on elementary school in-service teachers who have not had any experience or training in teaching English.
- This study investigated pre-service teachers during their teaching practicums.
- This study interpreted teachers' thinking using a qualitative approach.
- This study described lesson study conducted in Japan in English.

These points are addressed in the following ways. Regarding the first and second points, this study was driven by the fact that there is a lack of research on elementary school teachers who have not had any experience or training in teaching English. In addition, there is very little research on pre-service teachers, especially during the teaching practicum. I was able to describe their developmental process.

Regarding the third point, teachers' thinking is key to investigating teacher development. However, there is little research on teachers' thinking regarding teaching English (see Chapter 2, section 2.2.1). Consequently, the study contributes to that area. In addition, most previous studies were conducted using quantitative approaches regarding teaching English in elementary schools. I took a qualitative approach for this study. I provided participants the opportunity to have their voices heard in order to better understand their thinking. Furthermore, in this study, M-GTA was selected for analyzing the data. M-GTA is a version of GTA (Glaser & Strauss, 1967) developed by Japanese researcher Kinoshita (2003, 2007). M-GTA is well-known in Japan (see Chapter 3, section 3.4) and there is a lot of research using M-GTA. However, most of it is written in Japanese. M-GTA is not well-known internationally. Hence, the study contributed to introducing M-GTA outside Japan.

Concerning the fourth point, one of the purposes of the study was to document collaborative school-based lesson study conducted in Japan in English because although lesson study is spreading internationally, there are very few published studies of lesson study conducted in Japan in English. Researchers outside Japan have identified four aspects of conducting lesson study that pose challenges for U.S. schools: the time required for lesson study, the collaborative nature of the lesson study process, the need for common curriculum, and strong leadership. In Japan, time for lesson study is built into teacher work hours, and school norms provide opportunities for lesson study work during the school day (Fernandez & Yoshida, 2004). American teachers often work in isolation, managing lessons, curriculum, and students with little input from others (Slater & Trowbridge, 2000). On the contrary, Japanese teachers collaborate and share responsibility for student learning. American teachers use different textbooks, teach to different state and local standards, and use different teaching methods. In Japan, the national curriculum Course of Study facilitates lesson study work because all teachers in each grade level teach the same content, often through the same, or very similar, lessons (Lewis, 2000). Lesson study teams in the U.S. need strong leadership because team members are recruited and are not closely familiar with lesson study. A leader in the U.S. needs to attract members to the lesson study. On the other hand, Japanese teachers know lesson study well, and a leader only needs to facilitate the lesson study. Ultimately, this study, written in English, also contributes to the international literature on lesson study in Japan, where the concept originated.

8.5 Limitations of the study and directions for future study

This study is limited in that it analyzed a school in which ALTs have always been present. In subsequent research, I would like to investigate the developmental process of teachers engaged in school-based lesson study as implemented in schools that rarely have an ALT.

8.6 Concluding statement

This study investigated the developmental process of elementary school teachers associated with their experiences teaching English while engaged in school-based lesson study in Japan. The results have substantial implications for teacher development. Concerning pre-service teachers, the teaching practicum is the beginning of their acculturation into the teaching profession. They can somehow translate professional teacher knowledge into practice and foster a deeper sense of being a teacher during their teaching practicums. I would like them to keep learning collaboratively throughout their lifetime. Concerning in-service teachers, they can adapt knowledge and skills from other subjects for their English teaching. I would like them to have confidence and to keep learning with a positive attitude. In closing, I need to thank the pre-service teachers and in-service teachers who participated in this study. I am indebted to them for helping me understand teachers' development associated with their experiences teaching English.

References

A'Dhahab, S. M. (2009). EFL teachers' perceptions and practice regarding reflective writing. In S. Borg (Ed.), *Researching English language teaching and teacher development in Oman* (pp. 1-15). Muscat: Ministry of Education, Oman.

Allwright, D. (1998). Am I now, have I ever been, and could I ever be a developer? In M. Engin, J. Harvey, & J. O'Dwyer (Eds.), *Teacher training/teacher development: Integration and diversity* (pp. 138-143). Bilkent, Turkey: Bilkent University School of English Language.

Al-Weher, M. (2004). The effect of a training course based on constructivism on student teachers' perceptions of the teaching/learning process. *Asia-Pacific Journal of Teacher Education, 32*(2), 169-184.

Arnold, J. (1999). *Affect in language learning.* Cambridge: Cambridge University Press.

Aydin, S. (2016). Qualitative research on foreign language teaching anxiety. *Qualitative Report, 21*(4), 629-642.

Benesse Corporation. (2010). *Dai2-kai shogakko eigo ni kansuru kihonchosa* [The second basic survey of elementary school English].

http://berd.benesse.jp/global/research/detail1.php?id=3179

Benson, P. (2000). Autonomy as a learner's and teachers' right. In B. Sinclair, I. McGrath, & T. Lamb (Eds.), *Learner autonomy, teacher autonomy: Future directions* (pp. 111-117). London: Longman.

Borg, M. (2005). A case study of the development in pedagogic thinking of a preservice teacher. *TESL-EJ, 9*(2), 1-30.

Borg, S. (2003). Teacher cognition in language teaching: A review of research on what teachers think, know, believe, and do. *Language Teaching, 36,* 81-109.

Borg, S. (2006). *Teacher cognition and language education: Research and practice.* London: Continuum.

Borg, S. (2009). Exploring tensions between teachers' grammar teaching beliefs and practices. *System, 37,* 380-390.

Breen, M. P., Hird, B., Milton, M., Oliver, R., & Thwaite, A. (2001). Making sense of language teaching: Teachers' principles and classroom practices. *Applied Linguistics, 22*(4), 470-501.

Brewster, J., & Ellis, G. (2002). *The primary English teacher's guide.* Essex: Pearson Education Limited.

Burns, A. (1999). *Collaborative action research for English language teachers.* Cambridge: Cambridge University Press.

Burghes, D., & Robinson, D. (2009). *Lesson study: Enhancing mathematics teaching and learning.* London: CfBT Education Trust.

Burroughs, E. A., & Luebeck, J. L. (2010). Pre-service teachers in mathematics lesson study. *The Montana Mathematics Enthusiast, 7*(2&3), 391-400.

Butler, Y. G. (2004). What level of English proficiency do elementary school teachers need to attain to teach EFL? Case studies from Korea, Taiwan, and Japan. *TESOL Quarterly, 38,* 245-278.

Butler, Y. G. (2007a). Foreign language education at elementary schools in Japan: Searching for solutions amidst growing diversification. *Current Issues in Language Teaching, 8,* 129-147.

Butler, Y. G. (2007b). Factors associated with the notion that native speakers are the ideal language teachers: An examination of elementary school teachers in Japan. *JALT Journal, 29*(1), 7-40.

Cameron, L. (2001). *Teaching languages to young learners.* Cambridge: Cambridge University Press.

Carrier, S. J. (2011). Implementing and integrating effective teaching strategies including features of lesson study in an elementary science methods course. *The Teacher Educator, 46*(2), 145-160.

Carter, K., & Doyle, W. (1987). Teacher knowledge structures and comprehension processes. In J. Calderhead (Ed.) *Exploring teachers' thinking* (pp. 147-160). London: Cassell Education.

Charmaz, K. (2006). *Constructing grounded theory: A practical guide through qualitative analysis.* Thousand Oaks, CA: Sage Publications.

Chokshi, S., & Fernandez, C. (2004). Challenges to importing Japanese lesson study: Concerns, misconceptions, and nuances. *Phi Delta Kappan, March*, 520-525.

Clandinin, J. D., & Connelly M. F. (1987). Teachers' personal knowledge: What counts as personal in studies of the personal. *Journal of Curriculum Studies, 19*(6), 487-500.

Clark, C. M., & Peterson, P. L. (1986). Teachers' thought processes. In M. C. Wittrock (Ed.), *Handbook of research on teaching* (pp. 255-296). New York, NY: Macmillan Publishing Co.

Cohan, A., & Honigsfeld, A. (2007). Incorporating "lesson study" in teacher preparation. *The Educational Forum, 71*(1), 81-92.

Cowie, N. (2011). Emotions that experienced English as a foreign language (EFL) teachers feel about their students, their colleagues and their work. *Teaching and Teacher Education, 27,* 235-242.

Crawley, F., & Salyer, B. (1995). Origins of life science teachers' beliefs underlying curriculum reform in Texas. *Science Education, 79*, 611-635.

Creswell, J. W. (2005). *Educational research: Planning, conducting, and evaluating quantitative and qualitative research.* Upper Saddle River, NJ: Pearson Education, Inc.

Creswell, J. W. (2007). *Qualitative inquiry and research design: Choosing among five traditions.* Thousand Oaks, CA: Sage Publications.

Creswell, J. W. (2009). *Research design: Qualitative, quantitative, and mixed method approaches.* Thousand Oaks, CA: Sage Publications.

Creswell, J. W., & Miller, D. L. (2000). Determining validity in qualitative inquiry. *Theory into Practice, 39*(3), 124-130.

Curtain, H., & Dahlberg, C. A. (2010). *Languages and children: Making the match.* Boston, MA: Pearson Education, Inc.

Denzin, N. K., & Lincoln, Y. S. (1994). Introduction: Entering the field of qualitative research. In N. K. Denzin, & Y. S. Lincoln (Eds.), *Handbook of qualitative research* (pp. 1-17). Thousand Oaks, CA: Sage Publications.

Denzin, N. K., & Lincoln Y. S. (2003). *Collecting and interpreting qualitative materials* (2nd ed.). Thousand Oaks, CA: Sage Publications.

Dey, I. (2004) Grounded theory. In C. Seale, G. Gobo, J. F. Gubrium, & D. Silverman (Eds.), *Qualitative research practice* (pp. 80-94). London: Sage Publications.

Dobbs, K. (2000). Simple moments of learning. *Training Magazine, 37*(1), 52.

Dobson, R. L., & Dobson, J. E. (1983). Teacher beliefs-practice congruency. *Viewpoints in Teaching and Learning, 59*(1), 20-27.

Edge, J., & Richards, K. (1998). Why best practice is not good enough. *TESOL Quarterly, 32*(3), 569-576.

Ermeling, B., & Graff-Ermeling, G. (2014). Learning to learn from teaching: A first-hand account of lesson study in Japan. *International Journal for Lesson and Learning Studies, 3*(2), 170-191.

Fanselow, J. F. (1998). "Let's see": Contrasting conversations about teaching. *TESOL Quarterly, 22*(1), 113-130.

Farrell, T. (2007). *Reflective language teaching: From research to practice.* New York, NY: Continuum.

Fernandez, C. (2002). Learning from Japanese approaches to professional development: The case of lesson study. *Journal of Teacher Education, 53,* 393-405.

Fernandez, C., & Yoshida, M. (2004). *Lesson study: A Japanese approach to improving mathematics teaching and learning.* New York, NY: Routledge.

Fletcher, S. (2005). Integrating mentoring and action research into Kounai-ken: Teachers' professional development with Japanese abilities. Presented to the Annual Conference for the British Education Research Association.

Fosnot, C. T. (1996). Teachers construct constructivism: The center for constructivist teaching/teacher preparation project. In C. T. Fosnot (Ed.), *Constructivism: Theory, perspectives and practices* (pp. 175-192). New York, NY: Teachers College Press.

Freeman, D. (1989). Teacher training, development, and decision making: A model of teaching and related strategies for language teacher education. *TESOL Quarterly, 23*(1), 27-45.

Freeman, D., & Johnson, K. E. (1998). Reconceptualizing the knowledge-base of language teacher education. *TESOL Quarterly, 32*(3), 397-417.

Fullan, M. (1991). *The new meaning of educational change.* New York, NY: Teachers College Press.

Gardner, L. E., & Leak, G. K. (1994). Characteristics and correlates of teaching anxiety among college psychology teachers. *Teaching of Psychology, 21,* 28-32.

Gebhard, J. G. (1990). Interaction in a teaching practicum. In J. C. Richards, & Nunan, D. (Eds.), *Second language teacher education* (pp. 118-131). New York, NY: Cambridge University Press.

Gebhard, J. G., & Oprandy, R. (1999). *Language teaching awareness: A guide to exploring beliefs and practices.* New York, NY: Cambridge University Press.

Gifu JETs. (2010). Provisional translation from selected chapters of *Shogakko Gaikokugo Katsudo Kenshu Handbook (Teacher Training Handbook for Foreign*

Language Activities at Elementary Schools).

https://gifujets.files.wordpress.com/2010/03/eigo-note-guidebook-en-jp.pdf

Glaser B. G., & Strauss, A. L. (1967). *The discovery of grounded theory: Strategies for qualitative research*. New York, NY: Aldine Publishing Company.

Glaser, B. G. (1978) *Theoretical Sensitivity.* Mills Valley, CA: Sociology Press.

Glaser, B. G. (1992) *Basics of grounded theory analysis*. Mills Valley, CA: Sociology Press.

Glaser, B. G. (2005) *The grounded theory perspective III: Theoretical coding*. Mills Valley, CA: Sociology Press.

Golafshani, N. (2003). Understanding reliability and validity in qualitative research. *The Qualitative Report, 8*(4), 597-607.

Graham, P., Hudson-Ross, S., & McWhorter, P. (1997). Building nets: Evolution of a collaborative inquiry community within a high school English teacher education program. *English Education, 29*(2), 91-129.

Gratton, C., & Jones, I. (2004). Analyzing data II: Qualitative data analysis. *Research Methods for Sport Studies,* 217-227.

Gunstone, R., Slattery, M., Baird, J., & Northfield, J. (1993). A case study exploration of development in preservice teachers. *Science Education, 77*(1), 47-73.

Hatta, G. (1996). Teacher education research in ELT (IV): How do novice teachers differ from expert teachers? A study of teachers' thinking and learning. *Sugiyama Jogakuen University Bulletin, 27*, 83-93.

Hatton, N., & Smith, D. (1995). Reflection in teacher education: Towards definition and implementation. *Teaching and Teacher Education, 11,* 33-49.

Hiebert, J., Morris, A. K., & Glass, B. (2003). Learning to learn to teach: An "experiment" model for teaching and teacher preparation in mathematics. *Journal of Mathematics Teacher Education, 6*, 201-222.

Holt-Reynolds, D. (1992). Personal history-based beliefs as relevant prior knowledge in course work. *American Educational Research Journal, 29*(2), 325-349.

Horwitz, E. K. (1996). Even teachers get the blues: Recognizing and alleviating language teachers' feelings of foreign language anxiety. *Foreign Language Annals, 29*, 365-372.

Howey, K. R., & Zimpher, N. L. (1994). Non-traditional contexts for learning to teach. *The Educational Forum, 58*, 155-161.

Huang, J. (2007). Teacher autonomy in second language education. *CELEA Journal, 1*, 30-42.

Inagaki, T., & Sato, M. (1996). *Kodomo to kyoiku: Jugyo kenkyu nyumon* [Children and education: Introductory of lesson study]. Tokyo: Kitaohji Shobo.

Itoi, E. (2014). Pre-service EFL teachers' possible selves: Constructing stories of their profession. *JES Journal, 14,* 115-130.

Jadallah, E. (1996). Reflective theory and practice: A constructivist process for curriculum and instructional decisions. *Action in Teacher Education, 18*(2), 73-85.

Jackson, P. W. (1968). *Life in Classrooms.* New York, NY: Holt, Rinehart and Winston.

Jiang, Y., & Ma, T. (2012). A review of the research on language teacher autonomy. *Sino-US English Teaching, 9*(4), 1045-1055.

Johnson, K. E. (1994). The emerging beliefs and instructional practices of preservice English as a second language teacher. *Teaching and Teacher Education, 10*, 439-452.

Johnson, K. E. (1996). The role of theory in L2 teacher education. *TESOL Quarterly, 30*(4), 765-771.

Johnson, K. E. (1999). *Understanding language teaching: Reasoning in action.* Boston, MA: Heinle & Heinle.

Johnson, N. A., Ratsoy, E. W., Holdaway, E. A., & Friesen, D. (1993). The induction of teachers: A major internship program. *Journal of Teacher Education, 44*(4),

296-304.

Kagan, D. (1992). Implications of research on teacher beliefs. *Educational Psychologist, 27*, 65-90.

Kasuya, K., Hasegawa, T., Ito, I., Kimura, M., Shindo, S., Hazeyama, A., Kato, N., Narumi, T., Fujiwara, Y., Kurihara, S., Saito, Y., Hirata, Y., Yokoyama, A., and Furubayashi, S. (2014). Support of Foreign Language Activity of elementary school by using ICT (1): Analysis of the opinion poll among students of TGU. *Bulletin of Center for the Research and Support of Educational Practice, 10*, 81-89.

Kawakami, N. (2008). Training elementary school teachers in teaching English. *International Human Studies, 14*, 145-159.

Khan, S. (2014). Qualitative research method: Grounded theory. *International Journal of Business and Management, 9*(11), 224-233.

Khiat, H. (2010) A grounded theory approach: Conceptions of understanding in engineering mathematics learning. *Qualitative Report, 15*(6), 1459-1488.

Kinoshita, Y. (1999). *Grounded theory approach: Shitsutekijisshokenkyu no saisei [Grounded theory approach: Rebirth of qualitative empirical research]*. Tokyo: Kobundo.

Kinoshita, Y. (2003). *Grounded theory approach no jissen: Shitsutekikenkyu heno sasoi [Practice of grounded theory approach: Invitation to qualitative research]*. Tokyo: Kobundo.

Kinoshita, Y. (2007). *Live kogi M-GTA: Jissentekishitsutekikenkyuho, shuseiban grounded theory approach no subete [Live lecture M-GTA: Ways of practical qualitative research, Modified grounded theory approach]*. Tokyo: Kobundo.

Koehler, M. J., & Mishra, P. (2009). What is technological pedagogical content knowledge? *Contemporary Issues in Technology and Teacher Education, 9*(1), 60-70.

Kokuritsu kyoiku seisaku kenkyusho [National Education Policy Research Institute].

(2011). *Kyoin no shitsu no kojo ni kansuru chosahokokusho* [Report of teachers' quality improvement investigation] www.nier.go.jp/kenkyukikaku/.../kyouin-003_report.pdf

Kumaravadivelu, B. (l994). The postmethod condition: Emerging strategies for second/foreign language teaching. *TESOL Quarterly, 28*(1), 27-48.

Kumaravadivelu, B. (2001). Toward a postmethod pedagogy. *TESOL Quarterly, 35*(4), 537-560.

Kumaravadivelu, B. (2003). *Beyond methods: Macrostrategies for language teaching.* New Haven, CT: Yale University Press.

Kusumoto, Y. (2008). Needs analysis: Developing a teacher training program for elementary school homeroom teachers in Japan. *Second Language Studies, 26*(2), 1-44.

LaRossa, R. (2005). Grounded theory methods and qualitative family research. *Journal of Marriage and Family, 67*, 837-857.

Laskowski, T. (2009). Crossing borders in teacher development: *Jugyokenkyu* (lesson study) from the east and action research from the west. *Kumamoto University Bungakubu Ronso, 100,* 117-134.

Laskowski, T. (2011). *Jugyokenkyu* (lesson study) in America. *Kumamoto University Bungakubu Ronso, 102,* 59-77.

Leung, L. (2015). Validity, reliability, and generalizability in qualitative research. *Journal of Family Medicine and Primary Care, 4*(3), 324-327.

Lewis, C. (2000). Lesson study: The core of Japanese professional development. Paper presented at the AERA annual meeting.

Lewis, C. (2002). What are the essential elements of lesson study. *The California Science Project Connection, 2*(6), 1-4.

Lewis, C., Perry, R., & Murata, A. (2006). How should research contribute to instructional improvement? The case of lesson study. *Educational Researcher,*

35(3), 3-14.

Lewis, C., & Hurd, J. (2011). *Lesson study step by step: How teacher learning communities improve instruction.* Portsmouth, NH: Heinemann.

Lewis, C., & Tsuchida, I. (1998). A lesson is like a swiftly flowing river: How research lessons improve Japanese education. *American Educator, 22*(4), 12-17.

Lincoln, Y. S., & Guba, E. G. (1985). *Naturalistic inquiry.* Beverly Hills, CA: Sage Publications.

Liptak, L. (2005). For principals: Critical elements. In P. Wang-Iverson, & M. Yoshida (Eds.), *Building our understanding of lesson study* (pp. 39-44). Philadelphia, PA: Research for Better Schools.

Little, D. (1995). Learning as dialogue: The dependence of learner autonomy on teacher autonomy. *System, 23*, 175-181.

Lortie, D. C. (1975). *Schoolteacher: A Sociological study.* Chicago, IL: University of Chicago Press.

Machida, T. (2016). Japanese elementary school teachers and English language anxiety. *TESOL Journal, 7*(1), 40-66.

Magliaro, S., Murphy, S., Sawyers, J., Altieri, L., & Nienkark, L. (1996). *Reinventing teacher education: An examination of the social construction of learning in an elementary education program.* Paper presented at the meeting of the American Educational Research Association, New York.

Matsumiya, N. (2013). An attempt to foster future elementary teachers' English proficiency required to teach Foreign Language Activities: Investigating the potential of speech practice. *Bulletin of the Graduate School of Education, Hiroshima University Part 1, 62,* 81-88.

Matsumiya, S. (2013). A study on teacher concerns and teaching anxiety for primary school English education; An analysis and discussion of the issues: Construction and verification of English teaching anxiety models. *Kansai Gaidai University*

Journal of Inquiry and Research, 97, 321-338.

McKeon, D. (1998). Best practice: Hype or hope? *TESOL Quarterly, 32*(3), 493-501.

Merriam, S. B. (1998). *Qualitative research and case study applications in education.* San Francisco, CA: Jossey-Bass.

MEXT (2001). *Practical handbook for elementary school English activities.* Tokyo: Kairyudo.

MEXT (2007). *Shogakko ni okeru eigo-kyoiku ni tsuite* [English education in elementary schools].
http://www.mext.go.jp/b_menu/shingi/chukyo/chukyo3/siryo/015/07100309/005.htm

MEXT (2010). Course of study: Chapter 4 Foreign Language Activities.
http://www.mext.go.jp/component/a_menu/education/micro_detail/_icsFiles/afieldfile/2010/10/20/1261037_12.pdf

Moll, L. C. (1990). *Vygotsky and education.* Cambridge: Cambridge University Press.

Monoi, N. (2013). A survey on pre-service teachers' perception on Foreign Language Activities at public primary school. *Bulletin of the Faculty of Education, Chiba University, 61*, 9-14.

Morton, L. L., Vesco, R., Williams, N. H., & Awender, M. A. (1997). Student teacher anxiety related to class management, pedagogy, evaluation, and staff relations. *British Journal of Educational Psychology, 67,* 69-89.

Murase, M. (2007). Present status in practical research on education (1) Present status in lesson study. *Kyoikugaku Kenkyu [Education Studies], 74*(1), 41-48.

Murata, A., & Takahashi, A. (2002). Vehicle to connect theory, research, and practice: How teacher thinking changes in district-level lesson study in Japan. In *Proceedings of the twenty-fourth annual meeting of the North American chapter of the international group of the psychology of mathematics education,* 1879-1888.

Nagamine, T. (2011). Facilitating reflective learning in an EFL teacher education course: A hybrid/blended-learning approach. *Prefectural University of Kumamoto Bungakubu Kiyo, 17,* 13-35.

Nagamine, T. (2012). Preservice and inservice EFL teachers' perceptions of the new language education policy to "conduct classes in English" in Japanese senior high schools. *Afrasia Symposium Series Studies on Multicultural Societies, 2,* 123-139.

Nahatame, S. (2014). A survey of university students' awareness concerning English activities at elementary school: Focusing on students who aspire to be teachers. *JES Journal, 14,* 131-146.

Nakayama, H. (2011). A case study on the influences of Foreign Language Activities on teachers' consciousness at an elementary school: A case study of the teachers at "B" elementary school, in "A" city, Tokyo. *Mejiro Journal of Social and Natural Sciences, 7,* 47-59.

Nakayama, H. (2012). A case study on the influences of the in-service training about Foreign Language Activities on teachers' consciousness in an elementary school: A case study of the teachers at "C" elementary school, in "A" city, Tokyo. *Mejiro Journal of Social and Natural Sciences, 8,* 27-40.

Nakajima, S., & Okazaki, H. (2013). Qualitative research on Japanese elementary school teachers and assistant language teachers' perceptions about Foreign Language Activities: Transition of English learning from elementary school to junior high school. *Memoirs of the Faculty of Human Development University of Toyama, 8*(1), 181-199.

Nasrollahi, M. A., Krish, P., & Noor, N. M. (2012). Action research in language learning. *Procedia - Social and Behavioral Sciences, 47,* 1874-1879.

National association for the study of education methods (2011). *Lesson study in Japan.* Hiroshima: Keisuiha.

Neuman, W. L. (1991). *Social research methods: Qualitative and quantitative approaches.*

Boston, MA: Allyn and Bacon.

Nishida, H. (2006). Elementary school English education: The present condition of the Japanese education system. *Kansai University Forum for Foreign Language Education, 5*, 81-94.

Okazaki, H. (2012). English teacher reflective thinking based on student feedback. *Annual Review of English Language Education in Japan, 23*, 185-199.

Pajares, F. (1992). Teachers' beliefs and educational research: Clearing up a messy construct. *Review of Educational Research, 62*(2), 307-332.

Patton, M. (1990). *Qualitative evaluation and research methods.* Beverly Hills, CA: Sage Publications.

Pearson, J. (1985). Are teachers' beliefs incongruent with their observed classroom behavior? *Urban Review, 17*(2), 128-146.

Post, G., & Varoz, S. (2008). Supporting teacher learning: Lesson-study groups with prospective and practicing teachers. *Teaching Children Mathematics, 14*(8), 472-478.

Price, M. L. (1991). The subjective experience of foreign language anxiety: Interviews with highly anxious students. In E. K. Horwitz, & D. J. Young (Eds.), *Language anxiety: From theory and research to classroom implications* (pp. 101-108). Upper Saddle River, NJ: Prentice Hall.

Punch, K. F. (1998). *Introduction to social research: Quantitative and qualitative approaches.* Thousand Oaks, CA: Sage Publications.

Punch, K. F. (2013). *Introduction to social research: Quantitative and qualitative approaches* (3rd ed.). Thousand Oaks, CA: Sage Publications.

Richard, J. C., & Ho, B. (1998). Reflective thinking through journal writing. In J. C. Richards (Ed.), *Beyond training* (pp. 153-170). Cambridge: Cambridge University Press.

Richardson, V. (1994). *Teacher change and the staff development process: A case in reading instruction.* New York, NY: Teacher College Press.

Richardson, V. (1996). The role of attitudes and beliefs in learning to teach. In J. Sikula, T. Buttery, & E. Guyton (Eds.), *Handbook of Research on Teacher Education* (pp. 102-119). New York, NY: MacMillan.

Saiki, C. S. (2014). *Grounded theory approach wo mochiita data shushuho [Ways of collecting data using grounded theory approach].* Tokyo: Shinyosha.

Sasajima, S., & Borg, S. (2009). *Teacher cognition and language education.* Tokyo: Kaitakusha.

Segawa, T., & Fukumoto, M. (2006). Research on teacher education programs to facilitate reflective practicum: The analysis of inter-trainee collaboration and reflection. *Studies and Essays, 41,* 61-82.

Seidel, S., & Urquhart, C. (2013). On emergence and forcing in information systems grounded theory studies: The case of Strauss and Corbin. *Journal of Information Technology, 28,* 237-260.

Senior, R. M. (2006). *The experience of language teaching.* Cambridge: Cambridge University Press.

Sherman, A., & MacDonald, L. (2007). Pre-service teachers' experiences with a science education module. *Journal of Science Teacher Education, 18,* 525-541.

Shinato, Y. (2012). A qualitative study on elementary school teachers' awareness of Foreign Language Activities focusing on actual conditions. *JES Journal, 12,* 102-114.

Shön, D. (1983). *The reflective practitioner: How professionals think in action.* New York, NY: Basic Books.

Shön, D. (1987). *Educating the reflective practitioner.* San Francisco, CA: Jossey Bass, Inc.

Shulman, L. S. (1986). Those who understand: Knowledge growth in teaching. *Educational Researcher, 15*(2), 4- 31.

Shulman, L. S. (1987). Knowledge and teaching: Foundations of the new reform. *Harvard Educational Review, 57*(1), 1-22.

Simon, M. K. (2011). *Dissertation and scholarly research: Recipes for success.* Seattle, WA: Dissertation Success, LLC.

Slater, C. L., & Trowbridge, S. (2000). Master's level cohorts combat teacher isolation: University/school district collaboration. *Action in Teacher Education, 22*(1), 15-22.

Smith, R. C. (2000). Starting with ourselves: Teacher-learner autonomy in language learning. In B. Sinclair, I. McGrath, & T. Lamb (Eds.), *Learner autonomy, teacher autonomy: Future directions* (pp. 89-99). Harlow: Pearson Education.

Smith, R. C. (2003). Teacher education for teacher-learner autonomy. In J. Gollin, G. Ferguson, & H. Trappes-Lomax (Eds.), *Symposium for language teacher educators: Papers from three IALS symposia.* Edinburgh: University of Edinburgh.

Somekh, B. (1989). Action research and collaborative school development. In R. McBridge (Ed.), *The in-service training of teachers* (pp. 273-275). London: Falmer Press.

Stigler, J. W., & Hiebert, J. (1999). *The teaching gap: Best ideas from the world's teachers for improving education in the classroom.* New York, NY: The Free Press, A Division of Simon & Schuster Inc.

Strauss, A. L. (1987). *Qualitative analysis for social scientists.* New York, NY: Cambridge University Press.

Strauss, A. L., & Corbin, J. (1990). *Basics of qualitative research: Grounded theory procedures and techniques.* Newbury Park, CA: Sage Publications.

Strauss, A. L., & Corbin, J. (1998). *Basics of qualitative research: Techniques and procedures for developing grounded theory.* Thousand Oaks, CA: Sage Publications.

Suddaby, R. (2006). What grounded theory is not. *Academy of Management Journal, 49*(4), 633-642.

Tabachnick, B. R., & Zeichner, K. M. (1986). Teacher beliefs and classroom behaviours: Some teacher responses to inconsistency. In M. Ben-Peretz, R. Bromme, & R. Halkes (Eds.), *Advances of research on teacher thinking* (pp. 84-96). Lisse: Swets and Zeitlinger.

Tajino, A., & Tajino, Y. (2000). Native and non-native: What can they offer? Lessons from team-teaching in Japan. *ELT Journal, 54*(1), 3-11.

Takahashi, A. (2000). Current trends and issues in lesson study in Japan and the United States. *Journal of Japan Society of Mathematical Education, 82*(12), 15-21.

Takahashi, A. (2006). Types of elementary mathematics lesson study in Japan: Analysis of features and characteristics. *Journal of Japan Society of Mathematical Education, 88*, 15-21.

Takahashi, A. (2014). The role of the knowledgeable other in lesson study: Examining the final comments of experienced lesson study practitioners. *Mathematics Teacher Education and Development, 16*(1), 4-21.

Takahashi, A., & Yoshida, M. (2004). Ideas for establishing lesson study communities. *Teaching Children Mathematics, 10*, 436-443.

Tanaka, M., Honda, M., Osada, M., & Nishi, N. (2013). Implications from changes made for pre-service teacher training program for teaching English to children: From the perspectives of teacher cognition. *KATE Journal, 27*, 85-98.

Thompson, S. B. (2011). Sample size and grounded theory. *JOAAG, 5*(1), 45-52.

Tort-Moloney, D. (1997). Teacher autonomy: A Vygotskian theoretical framework. *CLCS Occasional Paper, 48.* Dublin: Trinity College.

Triwaranyu, C. (2007). Models and strategies for initial implementation of lesson study in schools. *International Forum of Teaching and Studies, 3*(3), 48-79.

Tschannen-Moran M. A., Woolfolk-Hoy, A., & Hoy W. K. (1998). Teacher efficacy: Its meaning and measure. *Review of Educational Research, 68*(2), 202-248.

Tsuji, N. (2010). Proposal for effective in-service teacher training of Foreign Language Activities in elementary schools. *Wakayama University Bulletin of the Faculty of Education, 60*, 89-95.

Uchino, S. (2015). What can university students learn about Foreign Language Activities?: A survey about the contents of university courses. *JES Journal, 15*, 83-94.

Wang-Iverson, P., & Yoshida, M. (2005). *Building our understanding of lesson study.* Philadelphia, PA: Research for Better Schools, Inc.

Watanabe, T. (2006). English for elementary school children: How to teach what and why. *Bulletin of Toyama Prefectural University, 16*, 73-80.

Watson-Gegeo, K. A. (1988). Ethnography in ESL: Defining the essentials. *TESOL Quarterly, 22*(4), 575-592.

Williams, K. E., & Andrade, M. R. (2008). Foreign language learning anxiety in Japanese EFL university classes: Causes, coping, and locus of control. *Electronic Journal of Foreign Language Teaching, 5*, 181-191.

Xu, H., & Pedder, D. (2015). An international review of the research. In P. Dudley (Ed.), *Lesson study professional learning for our time* (pp. 29-58). New York, NY: Routledge.

Yoshida, M. (1999). Lesson study [jugyokenkyu] in elementary school mathematics in Japan: A case study. Paper presented at the American Educational Research Association Annual Meeting, Montreal, Canada.

Appendices

Appendix 1 Selected analysis worksheet on pre-service teachers

Concept	<Guessing>	
Definition	Trying to understand English from gestures, expressions, and situations	
Examples	PST-A	I was impressed that the children guessed the meanings of English words without the teacher's translations or explanations. (Oct. 17, log)
	PST-B	The children could somehow understand English that they had not yet learned by understanding the situations. (Oct. 17, log)
	PST-E	Even if a teacher used slightly difficult English, the children could understand the meaning from the teacher's expressions and gestures. (Oct. 17, log)
	PST-D	Previously, I thought that children could not understand English without explanations or translations. Now, I know I was wrong about this. (Oct. 18, discussion)
	PST-B	The children were able to guess the meanings of English words from the teacher's gestures. It is important to make children guess the meanings of English words. (Oct. 18, discussion)
	PST-C	It is significant to develop the ability of guessing meanings. (Oct. 18, log)
	PST-D	Teachers should speak English almost all the time because children can understand English through teachers' gestures and expressions. (Oct. 18, log)
	PST-E	I understood that it was important to make children think about the meanings of English words through teachers' use of lots of English with gestures and expressions. (Oct. 18, discussion)
Theoretical notes	The children were learning English in an inductive way without explanations or translations. This is different from pre-service teachers' traditional ways of learning. Teachers should make children guess the meanings of English words.	

Appendix 2 Frequent words in the data of pre-service teachers according to KH coder Version 2

抽出語	出現回数	抽出語	出現回数
授業	214	中学校	14
英語	190	1つ	14
子ども	148	実習	13
活動	87	情報	13
考え	81	全員	13
時間	70	達成	13
コミュニケーション	51	聞き取り	13
自分	49	予想	13
発音	46	外国	12
先生	43	個人	12
目標	40	人	12
単元	39	反省	12
内容	37	意見	11
ゲーム	32	教科	11
教師	30	時刻	11
歌	29	ワークシート	10
表現	28	意味	10
指導	27	確認	10
意識	25	学習指導案	10
共同立案	25	共有	10
子	24	最後	10
学習	23	自信	10
指示	23	自身	10
次	23	助け	10
日本語	22	推測	10
友達	19	声	10
クラスルームイングリッシュ	18	単語	10
		本	10
不安	18	野菜	10
アルファベット	17	流れ	10
他	17	練習	10
文法	17	クラス	9
理解	17	ジェスチャー	9
アドバイス	16	音声	9
課題	15	感じ	9
クイズ	14	計画	9
外国語活動	14	検討	9
学習指導要領	14	実態	9

抽出語	出現回数	抽出語	出現回数
積極	9	相手	6
勉強	9	担当	6
机	8	注目	6
具体	8	発言	6
最初	8	反応	6
準備	8	文化	6
生活	8	目的	6
対応	8	あいさつ	5
中心	8	やり取り	5
定着	8	カード	5
働きかけ	8	チーム	5
導入	8	印象	5
様子	8	気	5
理由	8	教科書	5
やる気	7	教材	5
グループ	7	研究	5
ペア	7	現場	5
リズム	7	言葉	5
一面	7	好き嫌い	5
興味	7	高校	5
柔軟	7	指摘	5
重視	7	事前	5
上原	7	耳	5
身	7	実践	5
大学	7	整理	5
動作	7	素地	5
配分	7	他人	5
アンケート	6	体	5
イメージ	6	中身	5
学校	6	内	5
機会	6	難易	5
気持ち	6	日常	5
姿	6	不足	5
思考	6	方法	5
笑顔	6	連携	5
場面	6	シルエット	4
設定	6		
説明	6		

Appendix 3 Co-occurrence networks in the data of pre-service teachers according to KH coder Version 2

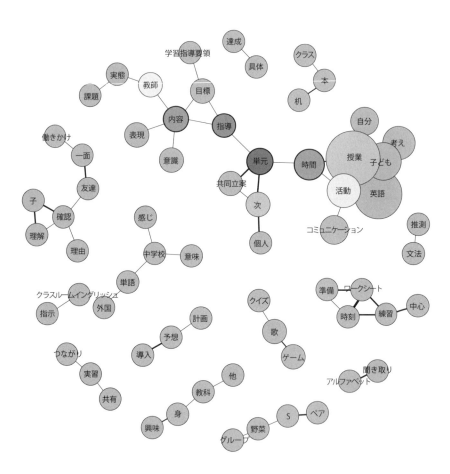

Appendix 4 Selected analysis worksheet on in-service teachers' views

Concept	<Ideal lesson>	
Definition	How they want to teach	
Examples	Teacher A	I would like to teach that learning English is interesting. I would like the children to communicate without hesitating. I want to be able to speak English and use a lot of English in lessons. I would like to communicate with the ALT well. (May 27, interview 1)
	Teacher B	The goal is to be able to make daily conversation in English, not grammar-translation. English at elementary schools is different from English education in secondary schools. It is important that the children become familiar with English. It is also important that the children like learning English. It is not good to translate English to Japanese. I would like the children to understand in English and react in English. (May 27, interview 1)
	Teacher D	I would like the children to think that speaking English is interesting. I want to grow my English competence in order to teach. (June 5, interview 1)
	Teacher E	The ideal lesson is one through which children learn English with joy. I would like to teach useful expressions. I want the children to like English for communication, not for entrance examinations. I would like the children to learn English through communication. (June 5, interview 1)
Theoretical notes	The ideal lesson is learning English through communication with joy. It is not the grammar-translation method.	

Appendix 5 Frequent words in the data of in-service teachers' views according to KH coder Version 2

抽出語	出現回数	抽出語	出現回数
英語	45	大変	4
授業	29	文法	4
自分	23	カリキュラム	3
子ども	13	クラス	3
先生	13	デモンストレーション	3
子	9	ブロック	3
学校	8	位置	3
指導案	8	意見	3
担任	8	感じ	3
一緒	7	環境	3
外国	7	企業	3
研究授業	7	協力	3
発音	7	校内	3
研究	6	姿	3
勉強	6	実践	3
流れ	6	書き方	3
ALT	5	身	3
イメージ	5	積極	3
コミュニケーション	5	素人	3
意識	5	単語	3
会話	5	中学	3
活動	5	統一	3
教育	5	日常	3
教材	5	不安	3
時間	5	やり方	2
主導	5	カード	2
専門	5	ノート	2
日本語	5	モデル	2
負担	5	意味	2
ダニー	4	夏休み	2
英語力	4	改善	2
学期	4	学年	2
教員	4	学力	2
経験	4	気持ち	2
研修	4	共通	2
参加	4	教科	2
主任	4	教科書	2
受験	4	教師	2

抽出語	出現回数
形	2
系統	2
語彙	2
公開	2
差	2
最後	2
市	2
思い	2
指導	2
塾	2
準備	2
小学校	2
人	2
世の中	2
政策	2
政府	2
戦士	2
選択	2
全員	2
全校	2
素地	2
打ち合わせ	2
単元	2
中学校	2
特例	2
日本	2
能力	2
配置	2
目標	2
役割	2
予算	2
立場	2
力	2
NO	1
OK	1
あゆみ	1
この辺	1
たたき台	1

抽出語	出現回数
まね	1
もん	1
やり取り	1
アップ	1
アンケート	1
イエス	1
イングリッシュ	1
エネルギー	1
ギャグ	1
グローバル	1
ゲーム	1
コントロール	1
センター	1
テーマ	1
バー	1
ビジョン	1
ファーストレディー	1
フレンドリー	1
マニュアル	1
メイン	1
ルーム	1
レディーファースト	1
案	1
1つ	1
一致	1
英	1
臆	1
音	1
音楽	1
音声	1
家庭	1
課題	1
会議	1
海外	1
害	1
各校	1

Appendix 6 Co-occurrence networks in the data of in-service teachers' views according to KH coder Version 2

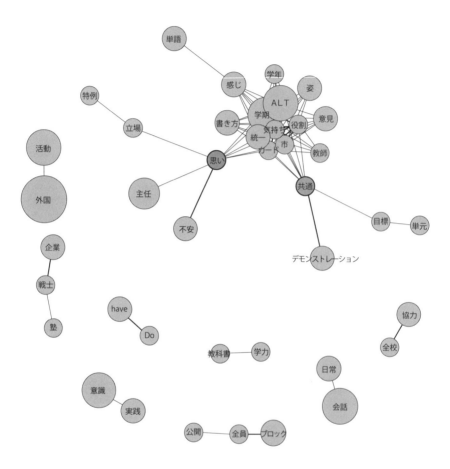

Appendix 7 Selected analysis worksheet on the developmental process of in-service teachers

Concept	<Critical views toward ALTs>	
Definition	See the ALT critically	
Examples	Teacher D	The ALT is supposed to join my class during other subjects. However, he always sits in the teacher's room. (March 10, Interview 2)
	Teacher B	Although he is supposed to come to classes during other subjects according to his contract, he does not come unless I ask. (March 10, Interview 2)
	Teacher A	I want the ALT to talk a lot in English with the children at lunch time, but he does not. He is kind, calm, and a very good person, but he rarely talks to the children outside of the lessons. I would like him to lead conversations with the children at lunch time. (March 15, Interview 2)
	Teacher C	The ALT speaks English too slowly sometimes. I would like him to speak naturally. He often gives answers to the children quickly. I want the children to think well, so I would like him to take some time. (March 11, Interview 2)
	Teacher E	The ALT moved to output activities quickly, but the children cannot perform output activities well without enough input. (March 15, Interview 2)
	Teacher B	I would like to give hints to help the children think well. The ALT does not have time to think. I began to think that the ALT was not an educator, and only an English native speaker. (March 10, Interview 2)
	Teacher B	I think that classroom control and making a unit topic attractive are the HRT's job. We do those things in other subjects, such as math, science, and social studies. An ALT is only a native speaker, not an elementary school teacher. (March 10, Interview 2)
	Teacher E	I began to think that I do not want to believe in an ALT too much. I would like to see ALTs critically. I am going to request anything to make lessons better for the children. (March 15, Interview 2)
	Teacher F	The ALT does not know the children individually very well, so HRTs should monitor the process of lessons and sometimes make requests to ALTs. (March 11, Interview 2)
	Teacher E	I came to think that an HRT's job was to observe the children carefully and request the ALT to teach according to the children's situation, and to create natural situations in which to use target expressions. My thinking changed after the research lesson. (March 15, Interview 2)
Theoretical notes	The teachers began complaining. The teachers realized that ALTs were only native speakers of English, and not teachers.	

Appendix 8 Frequent words in the data of in-service teachers' developmental process according to KH coder Version 2

抽出語	出現回数	抽出語	出現回数
英語	61	時数	4
授業	45	準備	4
子ども	34	上原	4
自分	30	声	4
先生	30	説明	4
子	19	発表	4
指導	18	文字	4
ダニー	17	勉強	4
打ち合わせ	15	あいさつ	3
教頭	13	あや	3
人	12	やり方	3
デモンストレーション	11	るい	3
最初	11	カリキュラム	3
研究	10	グループ	3
日本語	10	コミュニケーション	3
教科	9	メニュー	3
教材	8	学年	3
研修	8	活動	3
担任	7	感じ	3
流れ	7	機会	3
一緒	6	気	3
絵	6	教師	3
次	6	苦	3
発音	6	事前	3
学校	5	自信	3
環境	5	塾	3
専門	5	小学校	3
他	5	場面	3
まね	4	人数	3
カード	4	知識	3
クラス	4	日本	3
スタイル	4	附属	3
会話	4	名札	3
確認	4	理解	3
協議	4	力	3
検討	4	2つ	2
工夫	4	アドバイス	2
校内	4	イメージ	2

抽出語	出現回数	抽出語	出現回数
スキル	2	講座	2
ステップ	2	国語	2
テキスト	2	国際	2
ハイ	2	混乱	2
バージョン	2	最後	2
ビデオ	2	山口	2
プラン	2	子供	2
ポイント	2	市場	2
リズム	2	指示	2
レッスン	2	紙	2
意味	2	児童	2
1つ	2	耳	2
運動会	2	主導	2
英会話	2	週	2
科学	2	小口	2
絵本	2	場	2
外国	2	条件	2
確立	2	新田	2
学級	2	身	2
学生	2	進め方	2
感想	2	進行	2
観察	2	政府	2
丸	2	先取り	2
基盤	2	想像	2
記録	2	相談	2
共通	2	息	2
教室	2	大人	2
具体	2	単語	2
形	2	担当	2
経営	2	男の子	2
経験	2	中学	2
月	2	柱	2
見通し	2	内容	2
見本	2	年	2
原理	2	復習	2
口	2	雰囲気	2
甲府	2		
行事	2		

Appendix 9 Co-occurrence networks in the data of in-service teachers' developmental process according to KH coder Version 2

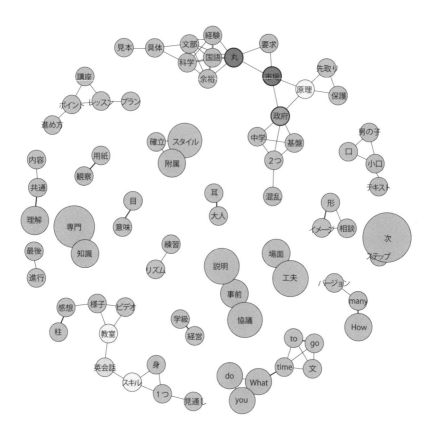

Index

A

action research 34-35

ALT (assistant language teacher) 17, 19, 53-54, 75, 88, 92, 98-101, 103-105, 110, 112, 114-135, 137-139, 142-147, 149, 151-153, 160-166, 168, 170, 172

Analytically-Focused Person 48

Analytical Themes 48

axial coding 42-44

C

categories 42-44, 46, 49, 52, 59-60, 102-104, 137-138, 141, 167

CK (content knowledge) 69, 156-158, 162, 168

concepts 22, 33, 43, 47, 49, 52, 58-60, 62, 69, 74, 77, 81, 102-105, 113, 116, 136-138, 142, 144, 148, 167

constant comparative method 41, 46, 50, 58

core-categories 49, 59-60, 102-104, 159, 167

Course of Study 17-18, 55, 59, 61, 77-81, 172

credibility 50-51

D

dependability 51

diagram 49, 52, 60, 104, 138

E

EFL (English as a foreign language) 22, 108

"Eigo Note" 18, 118

emic 39

epistemology 39

ESL (English as a second language) 22

etic 39

F

Foreign Language Activities 17-18, 25, 55, 60-61, 77, 79-81, 86, 100, 156

G

GTA (grounded theory approach) 40-42, 45-47, 171

H

"Hi, friends!" 18, 97, 118, 120, 150

I

interpretivist 38-39, 47, 50

J

JET (Japanese Exchange and Teaching) programs   17, 25, 29, 115

L

lesson study   11-16, 27-38, 45, 48, 55, 61, 81, 84, 87-90, 92-97, 99-
101, 119-121, 125-126, 131, 134, 139-141, 144-145, 148-149,
153, 155, 159, 161-165, 167-172

M

member check 52

methodological restriction 50

MEXT (The Japanese Ministry of Education, Culture, Sports, Science
and Technology) 17-19, 25, 29-30, 97, 100, 107-108, 111, 115-
116, 118, 133, 150

M-GTA (modified grounded theory) 14, 46-49, 52, 57, 102-103, 135,
167, 169, 171

MKO (more knowledgeable other) 28, 56, 61, 101, 125, 130, 159,
164-165

O

ontology 39

open coding 42, 46, 48-49, 59, 103, 137

P

paradigms 14-16, 38-39, 45

PCK (pedagogical content knowledge) 156-158, 162, 168

peer debriefing 50-52

Period for Integrated Studies 16, 79, 118

perspectives 14-16, 38-39, 45

PK (pedagogical knowledge) 156-158, 162, 168

positivist 21, 35, 38, 50

Q

qualitative approach 25, 40, 45, 47, 170-171

quantitative approach 40, 171

R

reliability 46, 50-52

Researcher-At-Work 48

research lesson 28-30, 56-57, 61, 89-96, 100-101, 120-122, 126-128, 131-132, 134-137, 147-148, 151

S

selective coding 42-44, 46, 48-49, 59, 103, 137

storyline 49, 52, 60-61, 104-105, 138-139

subcategory 43

T

teacher autonomy 24

teacher cognition 22

teacher collaboration 31-32, 35, 81

teachers' beliefs 23-24

teachers' thinking 14-16, 20-26, 37, 40, 45, 144-145, 169-171

theoretical coding 42

theoretical sampling 41, 46, 50, 52, 57, 102, 135

theoretical saturation 41, 44, 46, 50, 60, 103, 137

thick description 51-52

transferability 51

triangulation 50-52

TT (team-teaching) 53-54, 75, 92, 98, 103-105, 113-116, 120, 124, 133-134, 136-139, 141-144, 153, 160-161, 163-166, 168, 170

V

validity 46, 50-52, 137

W

WALS (The World Association of Lesson Studies) 31

Akiko Kambaru

Ph.D., is an Associate Professor of Teacher Education at Tsuru University in Japan. She has 23 years of teaching experience at elementary schools in Japan and the United States, and has been an instructor for teachers. Her major is teaching English to Japanese children. Some of her achievements are below:

Kambaru, A. (2017). Elementary school teachers' developmental process associated with teaching English in school-based lesson study. *JASTEC Journal, 37,* 103-118.

Kambaru, A. (2017). Jugyokatei to gakushushidoan no tsukurikata [Lesson procedure and how to make lesson plans]. In T. Higuchi, T. Kagata, E. Izumi, and T. Kinugasa (Eds.), *Shinpen shogakko eigokyoikuho nyumon [A primer of Elementary school English education, new edition]* (pp. 178-184). Tokyo: Kenkyusha.

Kambaru, A. (2007). Gakkoseikatsu no arayurubamende eigo wo tsukau kankyo wo tsukuru shogakkogakkyutannin no kokoromi [A challenge of an elementary school teacher to make an English environment in school]. *Dai 56 kai Yomiuri kyoikusho saiyushushojyushosha rombunshu [56th Collection of papers of the highest award winner of Yomiuri education prize],* 103-114.

The Developmental Process of Japanese Elementary School Teachers Associated with Teaching English while Engaged in Lesson Study

2019 年 2 月 9 日　初版発行

著者　　上原明子 かんばるあきこ

発行者　三浦衛

発行所　春風社 *Shumpusha Publishing Co.,Ltd.*

横浜市西区紅葉ヶ丘 53　横浜市教育会館 3 階
〈電話〉045-261-3168　〈FAX〉045-261-3169
〈振替〉00200-1-37524
http://www.shumpu.com　✉ info@shumpu.com

装丁　　長田年伸
印刷・製本　シナノ書籍印刷 株式会社

乱丁・落丁本は送料小社負担でお取り替えいたします。
©Akiko Kambaru. All Rights Reserved.Printed in Japan.
ISBN 978-4-86110-634-7 C3037 ¥5900E